Fodor's

New York City's
25Best

by Kate Sekules

Fodor's Travel Publications
New York • Toronto • London • Sydney • Auckland
www.fodors.com

How to Use
This Book

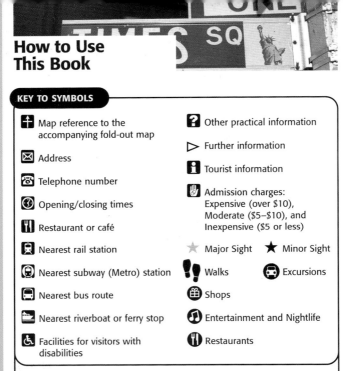

KEY TO SYMBOLS

➕ Map reference to the accompanying fold-out map

✉ Address

☎ Telephone number

🕐 Opening/closing times

🍴 Restaurant or café

🚊 Nearest rail station

🚇 Nearest subway (Metro) station

🚌 Nearest bus route

⛴ Nearest riverboat or ferry stop

♿ Facilities for visitors with disabilities

❓ Other practical information

▷ Further information

ℹ Tourist information

✋ Admission charges: Expensive (over \$10), Moderate (\$5–\$10), and Inexpensive (\$5 or less)

★ Major Sight ★ Minor Sight

👣 Walks 🚌 Excursions

🛍 Shops

🎭 Entertainment and Nightlife

🍴 Restaurants

This guide is divided into four sections
• Essential New York: An introduction to the city and tips on making the most of your stay.
• New York by Area: We've broken the city into six areas, and recommended the best sights, shops, entertainment venues, nightlife and restaurants in each one. Suggested walks help you to explore on foot.
• Where to Stay: The best hotels, whether you're looking for luxury, budget or something in between.
• Need to Know: The info you need to make your trip run smoothly, including getting about by public transportation, weather tips, emergency phone numbers and useful websites.

Navigation In the New York by Area chapter, we've given each area its own color, which is also used on the locator maps throughout the book and the map on the inside front cover.

Maps The fold-out map accompanying this book is a comprehensive street plan of New York. The grid on this fold-out map is the same as the grid on the locator maps within the book. We've given grid references within the book for each sight and listing.

Contents

ESSENTIAL NEW YORK   **4–18**

Introducing New York   4–5
A Short Stay in New York   6–7
Top 25   8–9
Shopping   10–11
Shopping by Theme   12
New York by Night   13
Eating Out   14
Restaurants by Cuisine   15
If You Like…   16–18

NEW YORK BY AREA   **19–108**
AROUND LOWER
MANHATTAN   **20–34**

Area map   22–23
Sights   24–30
Walk   31
Shopping   32
Entertainment and Nightlife   33
Restaurants   34

DOWNTOWN   **35–48**

Area map   36–37
Sights   38–43
Walk   44
Shopping   45
Entertainment and Nightlife   46
Restaurants   48

MIDTOWN   **49–70**

Area map   50–51
Sights   52–66
Walk   67
Shopping   68
Entertainment and Nightlife   69
Restaurants   70

UPPER EAST SIDE
& CENTRAL PARK   **71–88**

Area map   72–73
Sights   74–84
Shopping   85
Entertainment and Nightlife   86
Restaurants   88

UPPER WEST SIDE   **89–100**

Area map   90–91
Sights   92–95
Walk   96
Shopping   97
Entertainment and Nightlife   99
Restaurants   100

FARTHER AFIELD   **101–108**

Area map   102–103
Sights   104–107
Restaurants   108

WHERE TO STAY   **109–114**

Introduction   110
Budget Hotels   111
Mid-Range Hotels   112–113
Luxury Hotels   114

NEED TO KNOW   **115–125**

Planning Ahead   116–117
Getting There   118
Getting Around   119–120
Essential Facts   121–123
Timeline   124–125

CONTENTS

Introducing New York

"New York is an island off the coast of Europe." There's a lot of truth in this witticism, and it's no wonder this is the city most overseas visitors choose first. The qualities that weld New Yorkers to the city also mark them out as alien to heartland America.

Residents of Manhattan value directness, diversity and creativity; they live at a ridiculous pace; they work all hours (they have to, to pay the rent); they walk—fast—everywhere; they fail to keep their opinions to themselves; they have street smarts; they are capital L Liberal. Of the so-called Blue States—those dominated by Democrats—New York is the bluest of them all. The city that actually lived through the 9/11 attack that kicked off this era of paranoia and xenophobia, refuses to give into fear; New Yorkers have all the *chutzpah* they ever did.

Here, where some hip neighborhood is forever preparing to eclipse the last hot spot, change is the only constant. The crime-ridden, graffiti-scarred mean streets of the late 20th century are but a distant memory. In fact, terrorist threats notwithstanding, New York remains the safest large city in America, according to the FBI Uniform Crime Report. In stark contrast to the gritty days, you'll see Bugaboo strollers everywhere, because there is a mini baby-boom in progress. Real estate prices are in the realm of fiction, and a whole lot of regular folks have decamped for Brooklyn, while those who can't afford Brooklyn have gone to Queens. Harlem is all glamorous and beautiful; the Bronx is next. Staten Island, the fifth borough that most visitors know only for its fabulous ferry, is the final frontier.

But for many, Manhattan will always be the center of the universe. You can only take in so much of the big picture in one visit. So do as New Yorkers do—find a corner of the city and make it your own.

Facts + Figures

- **Visitors in 2008: 47 million (a record)**
- **Dollars spent by visitors: $32.1 billion (2008)**
- **Hotel rooms by end 2008: 76,000**
- **Eating establishments: 18,696**
- **New restaurants in 2008: 222**

REAL ESTATE

New York has not escaped the fall in property prices that has resulted from the sub-prime mortgage fiasco, credit crunch and the global economic downturn. Although, the city's real estate obsession continues with still hefty price tags; New Yorkers view their homes as not just their castles, but their portfolio, retirement plan and a chief financial burden.

BROOKLYN

Once a separate city, the vast borough across the East River has seen a migration of disaffected New Yorkers that has changed it forever. Once Brooklyn was unfashionable; now it's a Manhattanite's nighttime destination for restaurants, music and parties in those oh-so-desirable brownstones.

FREEDOM TOWER

Known as the Freedom Tower this 108-floor structure is the creation of architect Daniel Libeskind. In the north-west corner of the World Trade Center site and surrounded by memorial gardens, it is designed to be an imposing, striking and dignified memorial to the almost 3,000 people who lost their lives in the attacks on the twin towers of 9/11.

A Short Stay in New York

DAY 1

Morning Begin your day at 8.30 by taking the subway to **Grand Central Terminal** (▷ 58) and having breakfast in the splendid food court. Look at the main hall as you pass slowly through, then exit at 42nd Street and walk east to the **Chrysler Building** (▷ 52–53). Swing into the lobby, continue east through Tudor City to United Nations Plaza and walk north.

Mid-morning Stroll around the UN gardens by the East River, then take a tour of the **UN General Assembly Hall** (▷ 66). Double back on 42nd Street to Fifth Avenue and look in at the **New York Public Library** (▷ 61).

Lunch If it's summer, get something from the very good kiosks in Bryant Square or sit at one of Bryant Park Café's outdoor tables. In bad weather, eat inside the main restaurant.

Afternoon Walk a block and a half up Avenue of the Americas to the **International Center of Photography** (▷ 65) and after a quick viewing, head another block west to **Times Square** (▷ 64). Explore there, then join a line at the TKTS booth for discounted Broadway tickets.

Mid-afternoon Take Seventh Avenue up to 48th Street and go east, passing through the diamond district, to **Rockefeller Center** (▷ 62). Look around, then continue north up Fifth Avenue, passing St. Patrick's Cathedral to your right. For the rest of the afternoon, either shop **Fifth Avenue** (▷ 56–57) or head to **MoMA** (▷ 60) half a block west on 53rd Street. Or, if neither appeals, keep going up Fifth to **Central Park** (▷ 74–75).

Dinner Take up your early reservation at swanky **Casa Lever** (▷ 70).

Evening Enjoy whichever show you scored discount tickets for.

DAY 2

Morning Have a light breakfast at **Café Sabarsky** (▷ 88) in the Neue Galerie and be at the **Metropolitan Museum of Art** (▷ 80–81) when it opens at 9.30. Spend a while exploring the galleries.

Mid-morning Go back to the **Neue Galerie** (▷ 84), which opens at 11, and then squeeze in the **Guggenheim** (▷ 78–79). (Not ideal but at least you'll get a taste.)

Lunch Head over to Madison Avenue to **Jackson Hole** (▷ 88) for a burger, or if it's a beautiful day, leave enough time to enter Central Park at 85th Street and have lunch at the **Boat House** (▷ 88).

Afternoon Take the downtown 6 from 86th Street to Spring Street and do some shopping in SoHo. If shopping's not your thing, stay on the 6 (crossing the platform at Brooklyn Bridge, City Hall to the 4, 5) to Bowling Green, walk through Battery Park and board a ferry to the **Statue of Liberty** (▷ 26–27) and **Ellis Island** (▷ 25).

Dinner Dine at former speakeasy **'21' Club** (▷ 70) rubbing shoulders with the rich and famous in the Bar Room. Or if you thought far enough ahead, take your place at **Per Se** (▷ 70). If you did the latter, that is your evening.

Evening Walk up Broadway to **Lincoln Center** (▷ 94–95). If it's summer, take your dancing shoes to Midsummer Night's Swing on Josie Robertson Plaza; if not watch a performance in one of the many halls. Afterward, take in the late session at **Dizzy's Club Coca Cola** (▷ 99) back at Time Warner.

Top 25

American Museum of Natural History ▷ **92–93** Dinosaurs and the story of earth and space.

Brooklyn ▷ **104–105** No wonder everyone's moving there—it is an entire city unto itself.

Central Park ▷ **74–75** This large park has plenty of open space and activities to appeal to all ages.

Chinatown ▷ **24** The world's largest and still growing. Visit for the shops and restaurants.

Chrysler Building ▷ **52–53** Quite simply an icon and one of the world's most stunning skyscrapers.

Cooper-Hewitt National Design Museum ▷ **76** One of the largest design collections in the world.

East Village ▷ **38–39** A funky area of shops, ethnic diners and trendy clubs with plenty of history.

Ellis Island ▷ **25** The first landmark for 12 million immigrants between 1892 and 1924.

Empire State Building ▷ **54–55** The world's most famous skyscraper has the superb Observation Deck.

Fifth Avenue ▷ **56–57** Glamorous avenue with fashion shops, museums and landmark buildings.

Frick Collection ▷ **77** Striking masterpieces are displayed in Henry Clay Frick's mansion.

Grand Central Terminal ▷ **58–59** A railroad classic and much-loved attraction.

Greenwich Village ▷ **40** Trendy area crammed with shops, cafés, bookstores and cool bars.

Guggenheim Museum ▷ **78–79** Masterpiece of a building housing fine modern art.

Lincoln Center ▷ **94–95** The best in opera, music, jazz, ballet and theater is performed here.

Metropolitan Museum of Art ▷ **80–81** A spectacular collection spanning 5,000 years.

Museum of Modern Art ▷ **60** Painting and sculpture from the 19th century to the present.

New York Public Library ▷ **61** A beautiful Beaux Arts building with exhibits.

Rockefeller Center ▷ **62** A vital urban enclave in the heart of Manhattan.

Shopping Spree ▷ **63** If you were born to shop join the thousands who throng the streets daily.

South Street Seaport ▷ **28** A landmark district of historic buildings on the waterfront.

Statue of Liberty ▷ **26–27** The landmark is recognized across the world as a symbol of freedom.

Times Square ▷ **64** New York at its gaudiest— wild neon signs, big stores and theaters.

Union Square ▷ **41** A park, lots of restaurants, and the city's best green-market are here.

Whitney Museum of American Art ▷ **82–83** Major 20th- and 21st-century art lives here.

These pages are a quick guide to the Top 25, which are described in more detail later. Here they are listed alphabetically and the tinted background shows the area they are in.

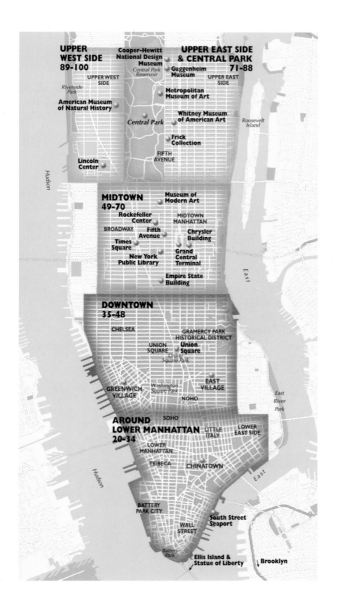

UPPER WEST SIDE
89–100

Cooper-Hewitt National Design Museum

UPPER EAST SIDE & CENTRAL PARK
71–88

Guggenheim Museum

Metropolitan Museum of Art

American Museum of Natural History

Whitney Museum of American Art

Frick Collection

Lincoln Center

MIDTOWN
49–70

Museum of Modern Art

Rockefeller Center

Fifth Avenue

Chrysler Building

Times Square

New York Public Library

Grand Central Terminal

Empire State Building

DOWNTOWN
35–48

Union Square

AROUND LOWER MANHATTAN
20–34

South Street Seaport

Ellis Island & Statue of Liberty

Shopping

Thought there was nothing you couldn't buy over the internet? Think again! New York is a shopping haven, with clothing, furniture, food and souvenirs available no place else. Shopping is still one of the best ways to get an inside look at life in New York—its trends, fads, pace, cultural influences and sense of humor. From massive department stores to small boutiques, the city has something for everyone.

A Piece of New York
You'll find all kinds of NYC paraphernalia—from Statue of Liberty coin banks and taxicab neckties to sweatshirts bearing the New York Police Department initials and Yankee baseball caps. Museum shops offer reproductions, posters, jewelry, stationery and commemorative items.

Fashion
For fashion head for Nolita and SoHo, where small (and often expensive) boutiques line the streets. Major franchises can also be found here, along Broadway, and side streets such as Prince Street, Broome Street and Spring Street. If you're planning a night out on the town, try the stores along 8th Street that are popular among young clubbers, starting on Broadway and heading west.

Music
Although the growth of download has seen the demise of many of the large music retailers,

---

WINDOW SHOPPING

No visit here is complete without window shopping. Start on Lexington between 59th and 60th streets: you'll see the flags outside Bloomingdale's. Walk west to Madison Avenue; between 60th and 61st streets is Barney's, for expensive clothing, jewelry, accessories and beauty products. Walk west along 57th Street, past Chanel and Christian Dior, to the prestigious Henri Bendel and Bergdorf Goodman stores. On Fifth Avenue peer in at Gucci, Tiffany's and Prada.

Shoes in a SoHo shop; sweet bread in Union Square; designer label in Chelsea; one happy shopper

there is still much to delight the enthusiast. Branches of Academy Records boast collections of vintage classical and rock vinyl and used CDs; Colony Music at 1619 Broadway is the original "if you can't find it here, give up"; or check out the Metropolitan Opera Shop (www.metoperashop.org) for something more classical. Note: DVDs cannot be played on European machines.

Bargains

If you're looking for a bargain, try the popular sample sales, where designer brands are marked down as much as 80 percent. Designer sales are often held at open showrooms over a few days. Arrive early on the first day of the sale for the best selection, though prices do drop as days go by. To learn about sample sales pick up *New York* magazine or *Time Out New York*, or log onto www.dailycandy.com. For electronic goods try J and R Music & Computer (✉ 23 Park Row ☎ 212/238-9000), plus other locations.

A Bite to Eat

As for food, in addition to the many upscale restaurants and cafés, simple NYC classics like hot dogs, pizza, bagels and frozen yogurt can be found on nearly every street corner, along with food carts purveying anything from hot soft pretzels or candied almonds to six kinds of curry or falafel sandwiches—great street food.

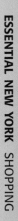

FLEA MARKETS

Bric-a-brac is at a premium in New York. You can find everything from silver and beaded jewelry to clothing, artworks and antiques at the Annex Antique Fair & Flea Market (✉ 125 W 18th Street (near Sixth Avenue), dawn–dusk every weekend, admission $1. Uptown, check out the huge GreenFlea market on Sunday, 10–6 (✉ Columbus Avenue between 76th and 77th streets). There is a Saturday GreenFlea market 11–7 in the Village (✉ Greenwich Avenue and Charles Street).

East Village outlet; Kors on Mercer Street; Dean & Deluca deli; glassware; Macy's at Christmastime

Shopping by Theme

Whether you're looking for a department store, a quirky boutique, or something in between, you'll find it all in New York. On this page shops are listed by theme. For a more detailed write-up, see the individual listings in New York by Area.

ACCESSORIES

Apple Store (▷ 68)
Di Modolo (▷ 85)
Laila Rowe (▷ 97)

BEAUTY

Bluemercury Apothecary & Spa (▷ 97)
Zitomer (▷ 85)

BOOKS

Barnes and Noble (▷ 97)
Kitchen Arts and Letters (▷ 85)
The Mysterious Bookshop (▷ 32)

CLOTHES

Abercrombie & Fitch (▷ 32)
Barneys (▷ 85)
Bergdorf Goodman (▷ 68)
Betsey Johnson (▷ 97)
Brooks Brothers (▷ 32)
Calvin Klein (▷ 85)
Cynthia Rowley (▷ 45)
Donna Karan (▷ 85)
Firefly Children's Boutique (▷ 32)

Hotoveli (▷ 45)
Jeffrey New York (▷ 45)
Malia Mills (▷ 97)
Marc Jacobs (▷ 45)
Ralph Lauren (▷ 85)
Resurrection (▷ 32)
Scoop (▷ 45)
Shanghai Tang (▷ 85)
Steven Alan (▷ 97)

DEPARTMENT STORES

Barneys (▷ 85)
Bergdorf Goodman (▷ 68)
Bloomingdale's (▷ 85)
Macy's (▷ 68)
Saks Fifth Avenue (▷ 68)
Takashimaya (▷ 68)

DISCOUNT

Century 21 (▷ 32)
DSW and Filene's (▷ 45)
Loehmann's (▷ 45)

FOOD AND WINE

Chelsea Market (▷ 45)
Fairway (▷ 97)
Gourmet Garage (▷ 32)
Greenmarket (▷ 45)
Kam Man Foods (▷ 32)

Whole Foods Market (▷ 68)
Zabar's (▷ 97)

HOMEWARES

ABC Carpet and Home (▷ 45)
Michael C. Fina (▷ 68)
Pearl River Mart (▷ 32)

SHOES

Alife Rivington Club (▷ 32)
DSW and Filene's (▷ 45)
Kenneth Cole (▷ 97)
Manolo Blahnik (▷ 68)

SPORTS GOODS

Nike Town NY (▷ 68)
Patagonia (▷ 97)

STATIONERY

Kate's Paperie (▷ 32)

TOYS

FAO Schwarz (▷ 68)

New York by Night

As the sun sets over New York, the city becomes at once a sultry, romantic and mysterious place. Wander through Times Square as the glitzy electric billboards pop out from the dark sky. A stroll, run or bike ride along the pedestrian path on the banks of the Hudson River on the West Side offers a spectacular view of the sunset and the Jersey shore.

Nightlife

As young New Yorkers explore new frontiers in the city, the Meatpacking District—once known for drugs and prostitution—has become home to trendy bars and clubs. Celebrity sightings are common at Spice Market (✉ 403 W 13th Street ☎ 212/675-2322) and 5 Ninth (✉ 5 9th Avenue ☎ 212/929-9460). At the other end of the spectrum are biker bars like Hogs & Heifers Saloon (✉ 859 Washington Street at W 13th Street ☎ 212/929-0655) and Fat Cat Billiards (✉ 75 Christopher Street in West Village ☎ 212/675-6056), friendly dives where the beer flows cheaply and the music blares loudly.

Take to the Water

Circle Line Cruises' evening boat rides around Manhattan are a relaxing way to see the world's most famous skyline. Board at Pier 83, at 42nd Street on the Hudson River (☎ 212/563-3200). Tour guides on board explain the legends of the city (www.circleline42.com).

Bright lights of Times Square and clubbers enjoying New York's nightlife

FOR A LAUGH

Comedy clubs are a great way to sample New York's sense of humor. Venues such as Caroline's (✉ 1626 Broadway, at 50th Street ☎ 212/757–4100), Upright Citizens Brigade Theater (✉ 307 W 26th Street, between 8th and 9th ☎ 212/366–9176) and Stand Up NY (✉ 236 W 78th, at Broadway ☎ 212/595–0850) are popular. The Laurie Beechman Theatre (✉ 407 W 42nd Street/9th Avenue ☎ 212/695-6909) hosts regular impromptu performances by the legendary Joan Rivers.

Eating Out

From basic diners serving trademark portions to über-trendy chefs, and from cafés showcasing world cuisine to the seriously fashionable, New York really can claim to offer something to suit every taste, diet and most budgets.

Around the World

Its global melting pot makes it almost impossible not to find just about every international cuisine in New York. Kosher, Polish, Italian, Greek and Chinese obviously have pride of place but you will also find everything from Afghan to Turkish, Argentinean to Russian. To get a real flavor of the city's culinary heritage check out a food tour such as those offered by New York Fun Tours (www.newyorkfuntours.com).

A Day's Dining

No one does "breakfast" or brunch like Manhattanites (especially at weekends) so make for Greenwich Village or SoHo, take your pick of establishments, grab a copy of the *New York Times* and just chill. For lunch, try a traditional Jewish deli for plenty of atmosphere and gargantuan sandwiches; make for the food court on the lower level of the majestic Grand Central Station or, if you're downtown, then Chinatown or Little Italy should help keep you fueled up for the rest of the day's shopping or sightseeing. Dinner in New York can be as casual or as stylish as your mood and budget dictates. Heading to a show? Then grab a pizza, steak or pasta in one of the many choices around and off Times Square.

TAXES, TIPPING AND FINANCIAL MATTERS

A sales tax of 8.875 percent will be added to your dining bill. The minimum tip (with good service) is 15 percent; many people double the tax for a 17.75 percent tip. Many restaurants offer prix-fixe menus, which are good value. In January and late June, a special promotion offers a three-course menu at reduced rates for lunch and dinner at numerous restaurants; this promotion is often extended so it's always worth checking if it's available.

Eating an ice cream; Costa Azzurra in Little Italy; hot dog; café at South Street Seaport; bagels

Restaurants by Cuisine

There are restaurants to suit all tastes and budgets in New York. On this page they are listed by cuisine. For a more detailed description of each restaurant, see New York by Area.

ASIAN

Fatty Crab (▷ 100)
Nobu (▷ 34)
Yama (▷ 48)

CASUAL

Barney Greengrass (▷ 100)
Boat Basin Café (▷ 100)
Bubby's (▷ 108)
Carmine's (▷ 100)
Jackson Hole (▷ 88)
Junior's (▷ 108)

CLASSIC

Le Bernardin (▷ 70)
Café Boulud (▷ 88)
Daniel (▷ 88)
Del Posto (▷ 48)
Gramercy Tavern (▷ 48)

CLASSIC NY

'21' Club (▷ 70)
Almond ▷ (48)
Boat House (▷ 88)
Four Seasons (▷ 70)
Katz's Deli (▷ 34)
Oak Room (▷ 88)
Odeon (▷ 34)
Oyster Bar (▷ 70)
Peter Luger (▷ 108)
Serendipity 3 (▷ 88)
Tavern on the Green (▷ 88)

COMFORT FOOD

Delicatessen (▷ 34)
Schillers (▷ 34)
The Spotted Pig (▷ 48)
Veselka (▷ 48)

CONTEMPORARY

Blue Ribbon (▷ 108)

Casa Lever (▷ 70)
Gotham Bar and Grill (▷ 48)
Grocery (▷ 108)
Jean-Georges (▷ 100)
The Modern (▷ 70)
Per Se (▷ 70)
River Café (▷ 108)
Thor (▷ 34)

EUROPEAN

Aix (▷ 100)
Café Sabarsky (▷ 88)
Civetta (▷ 34)
Double Crown (▷ 34)
Grimaldi's (▷ 108)
John's (▷ 70)
Ouest (▷ 100)
Picholine (▷ 100)
Sherwood Café (▷ 108)

MEXICAN

Mary Ann's (▷ 48)

If You Like...

However you'd like to spend your time in New York, these top suggestions should help you tailor your ideal visit. Each suggestion has a fuller write-up elsewhere in this book.

STAR CHEFS

Jean Georges Vongerichten's restaurant (▷ 100) is the flagship of his ever-growing worldwide empire.
Daniel Boulud at Café Boulud will wow you (▷ 88). Don't forget the madeleines.
Good luck scoring a table at Per Se (▷ 70). Thomas Keller has been called the best chef in America. Often.
For fish, nobody beats Eric Ripert at Le Bernardin (▷ 70).

CUTTING EDGE

Trot over to Jeffrey New York (▷ 45) to refresh your wardrobe, or for vintage, Resurrection (▷ 32).
Get a taste of the LES at the Parkside Lounge (▷ 33).
Have a late supper at The Spotted Pig (▷ 48).
Bed down at 60 Thompson (▷ 114), the Gansevoort (▷ 114) or, if broke, the Washington Square (▷ 111).

If you enjoy fine food, you w... love the choice and quality t... be found in New York (abov...

TO PARTY TILL DAWN

Friday and Saturday dance the night away to Latin grooves at S.O.B.'s (▷ 33).
Go with the groove at the late-night jazz series Friday and Saturday from 12.30am at the Blue Note (▷ 46).
Blue Ribbon is at its busiest late (▷ 108).
NYC's best cheesecake at 3am? Junior's! (▷ 108).

Classic views of New York, from on high (above right) and ground level, in the greenery of Central Park (right)

TIMES SQ

BIG AND BEAUTIFUL VIEWS

Harbor rooms at the Ritz-Carlton Battery Park (▷ 114) come complete with telescope.

Take in the lovely lake view from Central Park's Boat House (▷ 88)—unique in Manhattan.

Not everyone knows about the Roof Garden Café and Martini Bar (▷ 86) at the Met.

If you're not staying at Beekman Tower (▷ 112), visit the 26th-floor restaurant/bar.

Top of the Rock (▷ 62) rivals the Empire State Building (▷ 54–55) for the best view in town.

BRINGING THE KIDS

FAO Schwarz (▷ 68) is more than a store—especially since the renovation.

They won't believe the five-story indoor ferris wheel at Toys R Us, Times Square (▷ 64).

You can never go wrong with a zoo. Bronx Zoo is vast (▷ 106); the one in Central Park (▷ 74–75) won't take all day.

Take them to Serendipity 3 (▷ 88) for frozen hot chocolate.

Get tickets for The New Victory Theater (▷ 69).

CLASSIC NYC

See the ceiling, covered in toy trucks at the clubby '21' Club (▷ 70).

Bergdorfs, Saks and Bloomies are classic department stores with different personalities (▷ 68, 85).

The Chrysler Building (▷ 52–53) is New York's favorite skyscraper and an art deco masterpiece.

See how the other half lived at the Frick (▷ 77) and Cooper-Hewitt (▷ 76).

Bloomingdale's (top); view from the Empire State Building (above)

Entrance to the Bronx Zoo (above left); the famous spire of the Chrysler Building towers above the city (left)

SPORTING PURSUITS

Hope you're here in baseball season (April to September; post-season to October). Yankee Stadium (▷ 107) is a must. Or catch the Mets at Shea.

Madison Square Garden has it all (▷ 65, 69): basketball (the Knicks), boxing, tennis, track and field…

There's a game of something in progress in Central Park (▷ 74–75) all summer long. If it's winter, you can skate at Wollman Rink.

Shop for outdoor sports gear at Patagonia (▷ 97).

A LAUGH

See the comic legend Joan Rivers in intimate surroundings at The Laurie Beechman Theatre (▷ 69), which hosts regular spots by the acidic New Yorker.

A nongrungy stand-up venue: Gotham Comedy Club (▷ 46).

Score free tickets for a taping of *Saturday Night Live* or *Late Night with Jimmy Fallon* (▷ 62).

Look for whimsical artworks at MoMA (▷ 60) or the New Museum of Contemporary Art (▷ 29).

American sports and entertainment can be enjoyed year-round

PLACES TO BE SEEN

Thor is a showcase for people and the design of Marcel Wanders (▷ 34).

To spot models, try Schiller's (▷ 34) late.

The food is worth the wait for a free table at the Michelin-starred The Spotted Pig (▷ 48).

All Mario Batali's places are hot spots; his fanciest by far is Del Posto (▷ 48).

Taste a little of the Brooklyn scene at Sherwood Café (▷ 108).

Take time to dine out, the choice of good city restaurants is vast (right)

New York by Area

Sights	24–30
Walk	31
Shopping	32
Entertainment and Nightlife	33
Restaurants	34

AROUND LOWER MANHATTEN

Sights	38–43
Walk	44
Shopping	45
Entertainment and Nightlife	46
Restaurants	48

DOWNTOWN

Sights	52–66
Walk	67
Shopping	68
Entertainment and Nightlife	69
Restaurants	70

MIDTOWN

Sights	74–84
Shopping	85
Entertainment and Nightlife	86
Restaurants	88

UPPER EAST SIDE & CENTRAL PARK

Sights	92–95
Walk	96
Shopping	97
Entertainment and Nightlife	99
Restaurants	100

UPPER WEST SIDE

Sights	104–107
Restaurants	108

FARTHER AFIELD

The cradle of New York, Lower Manhattan has bags of history—new citizens in the 19th century first landed here—as well as the financial district, the historic seaport district and iconic Statue of Liberty.

Sights	24–30
Walk	31
Shopping	32
Entertainment and Nightlife	33
Restaurants	34

Top 25	TOP 25
Chinatown ▷ 24	
Ellis Island ▷ 25	
Statue of Liberty ▷ 26	
South Street Seaport ▷ 28	

Around Lower Manhattan

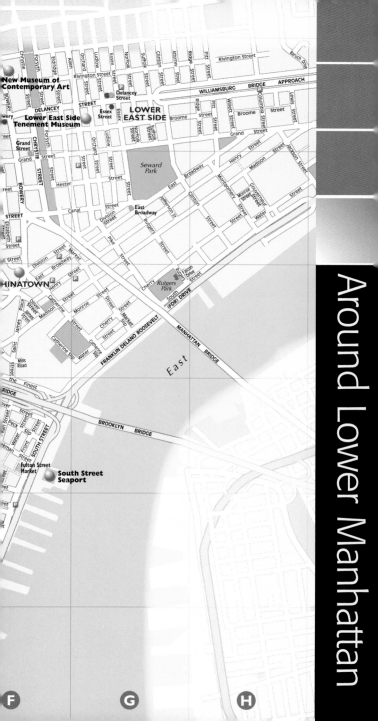

Chinatown

TOP 25

Streetlife in Chinatown (left and right)

THE BASICS

⊞ F20

✉ Roughly delineated by Worth Street/East Broadway, the Bowery, Grand Street, Centre Street

🍴 Numerous (some close around 10pm)

🚇 J, N, Q, R, Z, 6, A, C, E, 1, Canal Street; B, D Grand Street

🚌 M1, B51

♿ Poor

❓ General tours

www.explorechinatown.com

HIGHLIGHTS

● Buddhist temple (✉ 64B Mott Street)
● Chinatown History Museum (✉ 70 Mulberry Street)
● Pearl River Mart (✉ 477 Broadway, ▷ 32)
● Doyers Street: once the "Bloody Angle"
● Columbus Park (✉ Bayard/Baxter streets)

New York's Chinatown has swallowed nearly all of Little Italy and has spread over a great deal of the Lower East Side. Wander here and you're humbled by the sight of a lifestyle that thrives.

Going west Chinese people first came to New York in the late 19th century, looking to work for a while, make some money and return home. But, by 1880 or so, some 10,000 men—mostly Cantonese railroad workers decamped from California—had been stranded between Canal, Worth and Baxter streets. Tongs (bands of secret mafia-like operations) were formed, and still keep order over some 150,000 or more Chinese, Taiwanese, Vietnamese, Burmese and Singaporeans. New York, incidentally, has two more Chinatowns: in Flushing (Queens) and 8th Avenue, Brooklyn, with a further 150,000 or more inhabitants, but Manhattan's is the world's largest.

A closed world Although you may happily wander its colorful streets, you will never penetrate Chinatown. Many of its denizens never learn English and never leave its environs. The 600 factories and 350 restaurants keep them in work; then there are the tea shops, mah-jongg parlors, herbalists, and the highest bank-to-citizen ratio in New York, in which Chinese stash their wages (normally not more than $10,000–$20,000 a year) to save for the "eight bigs" (car, TV, DVD player, fridge, camera, phone, washing machine and furniture), to send home, or eventually to invest in a business of their own.

Ellis Island

Ellis Island at night (left); a Circle Line ferry passing Ellis Island (right)

This museum offers a taste of how the huddled masses of new immigrants were not allowed to go free until they'd been herded through these halls, weighed, measured and rubber stamped.

Half of all America It was the poor who docked at Ellis Island after sometimes grueling voyages in steerage, since first-class passage included permission to decant straight into Manhattan. Annie Moore, aged 15 and the first immigrant to disembark here, arrived in 1892, followed by 16 million immigrants over the next 40 years, including such then-fledgling Americans as Irving Berlin and Frank Capra. Half the population of the United States can trace their roots to an Ellis Island immigrant.

Island of Tears The exhibition in the main building conveys the indignities, frustrations and fears of the arrivals. (As you arrive, collect your free ticket for the half-hour film, *Island of Hope/Island of Tears*, or you'll miss it.) You are guided around more or less the same route new arrivals took: from the Baggage Room, where they had to abandon all they owned; onward to the large Registry Room, now bare of furniture; and through the inspection chambers where medical, mental and political status were ascertained. The Oral History Studio brings it all to life as immigrants recount their experience—especially moving when coupled with the poignant items in the "Treasures from Home" exhibit. This is a demanding few hours' sightseeing. Wear sensible shoes and bring lunch.

THE BASICS

www.ellisisland.org

✚ Off map at E23

✉ Ellis Island

☎ 212/363–3200

🕐 Daily 9–5.15; closed 25 Dec

🍴 Café

🚇 4, 5 Bowling Green, South Ferry, then take ferry

🚌 M1, M6, M15 South Ferry, then take the ferry

🛳 Ferry departs Battery Park South Ferry every 30 mins. Ferry information ☎ 877/523-9849; www.statuecruises.com

♿ Good

💵 Museum free; ferry expensive

❓ Audio tours available

HIGHLIGHTS

- Wall of Honor
- Treasures from Home
- Oral History Studio
- Dormitory
- Through America's Gate
- View of Lower Manhattan

Statue of Liberty

TOP 25

- View from the crown
- Statue of Liberty Museum
- Fort Wood, the star-shape pedestal base
- Her new centenary flame

TIP

- Visits to the crown have to be reserved in advance on tel: 877/523-9849; www.statuecruises.com

The green lady, symbol of the American dream of freedom, takes your breath away, however many times you've seen her photograph—and despite her surprisingly modest stature.

How she grew In the late 1860s, sculptor Frédéric-Auguste Bartholdi dreamed of placing a monument to freedom in a prominent location. His dream merged with the French historian Edouard-René de Laboulaye's idea of presenting the American people with a statue that celebrated freedom and the two nations' friendship. Part of the idea was to shame the repressive French government, but, apparently, New Yorkers took their freedom for granted: It was only after Joseph Pulitzer promised to print the name of every donor in his newspaper, the *New York World*, that

Clockwise from left: tourists posing at the base of the Statue of Liberty; Liberty seen on her island; detail of one of the most famous statues in the world; a coin-operated lookout point for viewing the Statue of Liberty

THE BASICS

www.nps.gov/stli

✚ Off map at E23

✉ Liberty Island

☎ 212/363-3200

🕐 Daily 9.30–5; extended hours in peak season. A limited number of daily tickets to tour the monument may be reserved in advance from ferry office, by phone or online

🍴 Cafeteria

🚇 4, 5 Bowling Green, South Ferry, then take ferry

🚌 M1, M6, M15 South Ferry, then take ferry

⛴ Departs Battery Park South Ferry (AF19)

☎ 877/523-9849; www.statuecruises.com

♿ Poor

💵 Free; ferry expensive

the city's citizens coughed up the funds to build the pedestal. Liberty was unveiled by President Grover Cleveland on October 28, 1886.

Mother of exiles Emma Lazarus' stirring poem, *The New Colossus*, is engraved on the pedestal, while the tablet reads: July IV MDCCLXXVI—the date of the Declaration of Independence. Beneath her size 107 feet, she tramples the shackles of tyranny, and her seven-pointed crown beams liberty to the seven continents and the seven seas.

What is she made of? Gustave Eiffel practiced for his later work by designing the 1,700-bar iron and steel structure that supports her. She weighs 225 tons, is 151ft (46m) tall, has an 8ft (2m) index finger and a skin of 300 copper plates. The torch tip towers 305ft (93m) above sea level.

South Street Seaport

The skyline behind the seaport (left); entertainment for visitors (right)

THE BASICS

www.southstseaport.org

⊞ F21

✉ Visitor center: 12 Fulton Street. Tickets also from Pier 16

☎ 212/748–8600

🕐 Most shops Mon–Sat 10–9, Sun 11–8; Museum Apr–Oct Tue–Sun 10–6; Nov–Mar Fri–Sun 10–5, ships 12–5. Also Schermerhorn Row galleries only on Mon 10–5. Closed Dec 25 and Jan 1

🍴 Numerous

🚇 2, 3, 4, 5, J, Z Fulton Street; A, C Broadway-Nassau Street

🚌 M15 Pearl/Fulton Street

♿ Poor

💲 Moderate

HIGHLIGHTS

● View of Brooklyn Heights
● Richard Haas' Brooklyn Bridge mural
● The historic buildings of Schermerhorn Row
● Boarding *Andrew Fletcher*
● Titanic Memorial
● Chandlery
● Fulton Market (especially the bakeries)

This reconstructed historic maritime district, with its cobbled streets, is a tourist trap. However, when you stroll the boardwalk on a summer's night, with the moon over the East River, you are very glad to be a tourist.

Pier, cruise, shop, eat The seaside/cruise-ship atmosphere is what's fun at the Pier 17 Pavilion, which juts 400ft (122m) into the East River, overlooking Brooklyn Heights. It's a mall, with chain stores, bad restaurants and a food court, but also three stories of charming wooden decks. The adjoining piers, 16 and 15, harbor a number of historic vessels with picturesque arrangements of rigging, as well as the replica side-wheeler *Andrew Fletcher* and the 1885 schooner *Pioneer*, which give harbor cruises. Your cash is courted by many stores, housed in the 1812 Federal-style warehouses of Schermerhorn Row—Manhattan's oldest block—and around Water, Front and Fulton streets, and by the cafés in the old Fulton Market.

Many museums The Seaport Museum Visitors' Center acts as clearing house for all the small-scale exhibitions here. One ticket admits you to the second-biggest sailing ship ever built, the *Peking*; the floating lighthouse, Ambrose; the Children's Center; the Seaport Museum Gallery; a re-creation of a 19th-century printer's shop; various walking tours (including "Ship Restoration" and "Back Streets"—worthwhile if you have the time) and more.

More to See

BATTERY PARK
www.thebattery.org
This refuge for workers in the Financial District was named for the cannon sited here to defend the fledgling city against British attack. Buy tickets for the Statue of Liberty at Castle Clinton.
➕ E23 ✉ Tip of Manhattan 🚇 1, South Ferry; 4, 5 Bowling Green

CHILDREN'S MUSEUM OF THE ARTS
www.cmany.org
Highlights include the Monet Ballpond, Architects Alley and Wonder Theater.
➕ E18/19 ✉ 182 Lafayette Street ☎ 212/274-0986 🕐 Wed, Fri–Sun 12–5, Thu 12–6 🚇 6 Spring Street 💲 Moderate

CITY HALL
French Renaissance-style facade and elegant Georgian interior—see it by visiting the Governor's Room, with a small furniture museum.
➕ E20 ✉ Broadway/Murray Street ☎ 212/788–3000 🕐 Mon–Fri 10–3.30 🚇 2, 3 Park Place; 4, 5, 6 Brooklyn Bridge-City Hall; N, R City Hall 💲 Free

GROUND ZERO
www.wtcprogress.com
Work is under way on the Freedom Tower (▷ 5), a 108-floor construction on the site of the former twin towers. Completion dates vary (see website).
➕ D21 ✉ Church to West streets, Liberty to Vesey streets 🚇 E World Trade Center

LOWER EAST SIDE TENEMENT MUSEUM
www.tenement.org
This reconstruction of life in an 1863 tenement block is a must for history buffs. Intriguing tours and talks.
➕ G18 ✉ 108 Orchard Street ☎ 212/982-8420 🕐 Tours daily 10–5 🚇 F, J, Z Delancey Street; B, D, Q Grand Street 💲 Expensive

NEW MUSEUM OF CONTEMPORARY ART
www.newmuseum.org
A striking white, modern building houses this cutting-edge museum.
➕ F18 ✉ 235 Bowery/Prince Street ☎ 212/219–1222 🕐 Wed–Sun 12–6, Thu–Fri 12–10 🚇 N, R Prince Street 💲 Expensive

A poignant tribute at Ground Zero

World Trade Center Globe Statue Memorial, Battery Park

NEW YORK CITY POLICE MUSEUM

www.nycpolicemuseum.org

A small museum with a wealth of cops and robbers material including handguns, uniforms and shields. Visit a prison cell and learn about forensics. The NYPD Hall of Heroes has a memorial to the heroes who died on 9/11.

⊞ F22 ✉ 100 Old Slip ☎ 212/480–3100 🕐 Mon–Sat 10–5 🚇 2, 3 Wall Street ✋ Donation suggested, moderate

NEW YORK STOCK EXCHANGE

www.nyse.com

The neoclassical facade dates only from 1903. The Stock Exchange is not currently open for visits or tours. Telephone for up-to-date information.

⊞ E22 ✉ 20 Broad Street ☎ 212/656–3000 🚇 2, 3, 4, 5 Wall Street; J, Z Broad Street

ST. PATRICK'S OLD CATHEDRAL

www.oldcathedral.org

New York's first Roman Catholic cathedral opened in 1815, when the area was settled by Irish immigrants. The original structure was destroyed by fire in 1866, but enlarged and rebuilt by 1868. When the new St. Pat's (▷ 66) was built in 1879, the cathedral became a parish church.

⊞ F18 ✉ 263 Mulberry Street ☎ 212/226-8075 (call for times) 🚇 N R, Q Prince Street

SINGER BUILDING AND HAUGHWOUT BUILDING

www.sohonyc.com

Two of the best ambassadors for the SoHo Cast Iron Historic District—the 26 blocks of skyscraper forerunners, now galleries and upscale boutiques. The Haughwout had the first Otis steam elevator.

⊞ E18 ✉ Singer: 561 Broadway. Haughwout: 488 Broadway 🚇 N, R Prince Street; F, B, D Broadway-Lafayette Street

WOOLWORTH BUILDING

The world's tallest until the Chrysler, Cass Gilbert's Gothic beauty has NYC's richest lobby—with witty bas reliefs of Gilbert and tycoon F. W. Woolworth. Closed to the public.

⊞ E21 ✉ 233 Broadway 🚇 2, 3 Park Place; N, R City Hall

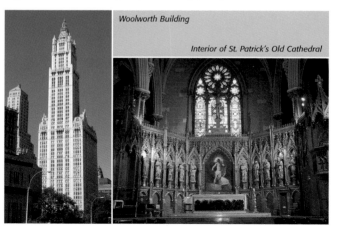

Woolworth Building

Interior of St. Patrick's Old Cathedral

Lower Manhattan to Downtown

An ideal introduction to Lower Manhattan from the tip of Broadway to the heart of Greenwich Village via City Hall, Little Italy and SoHo.

DISTANCE: 2 miles (3km) **ALLOW:** 40 minutes

START

CHURCH STREET
✚ E21 🚇 2, 3 Park Place

END

GREENWICH VILLAGE (▷ 40)
✚ C17 🚇 A, B, C, D, E, F, M W 4th Street

❶ Walk east on Barclay Street, turn left onto Broadway and look to your left for the Woolworth Building. At City Hall Park continue along Broadway, where City Hall comes into view on your right.

❷ Walk east through the park and catch a vista of Brooklyn Bridge. Continue north up Centre Street to Cass Gilbert's US Courthouse on Foley Square.

❸ The neoclassical New York County Courthouse is past Pearl Street on the right, and then, past Hogan Place, the Criminal Courts (The Tombs).

❹ Another block, and here's Canal Street. Go east to Mulberry Street. Continue north through Little Italy and veer west on Prince Street to the Cast Iron Historic District of SoHo.

❽ Keep heading west to expore the Village further.

❼ Fifth Avenue starts at the north side. Look at gated Washington Square Mews (first right), turn left on W 8th Street (see MacDougal Alley, first left) to Avenue of the Americas (6th Avenue).

❻ Take any route west through the streets of SoHo, heading north across Houston Street anywhere from Mercer to MacDougal; now you're in Greenwich Village. Three blocks north, you reach Washington Square, the center of New York University.

❺ Look at the Singer Building opposite as you cross Broadway.

Shopping

ABERCROMBIE & FITCH
Teens and college grads are the core customers at this temple to slouchy American style, famous for its rather racy Bruce Weber-shot catalogs. The clothes, though, are good for anyone's weekends and the prices are gentle. There are men's and women's lines.
➕ F21 ✉ 199 Water Street/Fulton Street ☎ 212/809-9000 🚇 2, 3, 4, 5, A, C, J, Z Fulton Street-Broadway-Nassau

ALIFE RIVINGTON CLUB
Here behind an unmarked door, trainers are high fashion, with all the latest footwear from American, European and Japanese lines. Great colors and limited editions are available.
➕ G18 ✉ 158 Rivington Street, between Clinton and Suffolk streets ☎ 212/375-8128 🚇 F, J, Z Delancey Street/Essex Street

BROOKS BROTHERS
Home of the preppy, Brooks Brothers also caters to anyone, male or female (though the men's department is far better) who wants to look pulled together. Their basics, like boxer shorts and white dress shirts, are exceptional.
➕ E21 ✉ 1 Church Street/Liberty Plaza ☎ 212/267-2400 🚇 4, 5 Fulton Street

CENTURY 21
Practically a cult, especially in the European designer area.
➕ E21 ✉ 22 Cortlandt Street ☎ 212/227-9092 🚇 4, 5 Fulton Street

FIREFLY CHILDREN'S BOUTIQUE
Two-store boutique with high-quality children's clothing and educational toys. A good place to pick up something unusual and non-mass market.
➕ 21 ✉ 224 Front Street, South Street Seaport ☎ 646/416-6560 🚇 2, 3, 4, 5, A, C, J, Z Fulton Street

GOURMET GARAGE
The place to find yellow cherry tomatoes, dried cherries, fresh clams, truffle butter, smoked duck, gelati, you-name-it.
➕ E18 ✉ 435 Broome Street/Mercer Street

PEARL RIVER MART

Shop here for chrome lunch pails with clip-on lids; embroidered silk pajamas and Suzy Wong dresses; bamboo fans and porcelain rice bowls—all the things, in fact, you can get in the smaller Chinatown emporia, but collected under one roof. The food department sells an eclectic range. The prices are very, very low.
➕ E18 ✉ 477 Broadway (Broome Street) ☎ 212/431-4770 🚇 N, R Canal Street

---

☎ 212/941-5850 🚇 N, R Prince Street

KAM MAN FOODS
This large Chinese food store overflows with exotic products, from live fish and edible birds' nests to ginseng priced at hundreds of dollars. Also Asian cookware.
➕ F19 ✉ 200 Canal Street/Mott Street ☎ 212/571-0330 🚇 J, Z Canal Street

KATE'S PAPERIE
The beautiful handmade stationery is overwhelming at this SoHo boutique.
➕ E18 ✉ 72 Spring Street, between Crosby and Lafayette streets ☎ 212/941-9816 🚇 6 Spring Street

THE MYSTERIOUS BOOKSHOP
A must for mystery lovers. Staff will lead you to new discoveries alongside famous writers from Raymond Chandler to Patricia Highsmith. Rare volumes and first editions.
➕ E20 ✉ 58 Warren Street/Church Street ☎ 212/587-1011 🚇 1, 2, 3, A, C, E Chambers Street

RESURRECTION
A haul of pricey but perfect vintage, with an emphasis on collectible labels: Pucci, Halston, Courrèges, Dior. The owners offer their own line of skirts and tops.
➕ F18 ✉ 217 Mott Street, between Spring and Prince streets ☎ 212/625-1374 🚇 6 Spring Street

Entertainment and Nightlife

ARLENE'S GROCERY
www.arlenesgrocery.net
One of the best rock clubs in the city, where hot new bands make their name.
🔴 G18 ✉ 95 Stanton Street, between Ludlow and Orchard streets ☎ 212/995-1652 Ⓜ F, M 2nd Avenue

BARRAMUNDI
www.barramundiny.com
Woodsy decor, a neighborhood crowd, Aussie beers and a new flavor of infused vodka every week are among the draws at this Lower East Side hangout.
🔴 G18 ✉ 67 Clinton Street near Rivington Street ☎ 212/529-6999 Ⓜ F, J, Z Delancey Street-Essex Street

BEACH AT GOVERNORS ISLAND
www.thebeachconcerts.com
Outdoor venue for live events with bars, café and beer garden. Enjoy views of the Manhattan skyline as you boogie to DJs and big-name bands.
🔴 Off map ✉ Governors Island ☎ No phone 🚢 Water Taxi from Battery Maritime Building Slip at 10 South Street

BECKETT'S
www.beckettsnyc.com
Many a Wall Street worker can be seen here mulling over the meltdown in the financial world. The popular outdoor seating area is open April to November. 18 giant screens show your favorite games.
🔴 E22 ✉ 81 Pearl Street ☎ 212/269-1001 Ⓜ 2, 3 Wall Street

BRIDGE CAFÉ
This loveable place has been serving continuously since 1794—yes it's one of the oldest taverns in town. The bar is a lovely place to end an evening after a stroll by the water.
🔴 F21 ✉ 279 Water Street/Dover Street ☎ 212/227-3344 Ⓜ 4, 5, 6 Brooklyn Bridge-City Hall

COMEDY CELLAR
www.comedycellar.com
Cozy Greenwich Village spot where frequently established comedians appear from time to time. Intimate nature of the venue means you are quite likely to find you are part of the show.
🔴 17 ✉ 117 MacDougal Street, between W 3rd Street and Minetta Lane

☎ 212/254-3480 Ⓜ A, B, C, D, E, F, M 4th Street/Washington Square

PARKSIDE LOUNGE
www.parksidelounge.net
A multipurpose venue that hosts live music, stand-ups and karaoke, and people having a beer. It's open until 4am. An unpretentious minimally art-directed place to sample the Lower East Side buzz.
🔴 G17 ✉ 317 E Houston Street/Attorney Avenue ☎ 212/673-6270 Ⓜ F, M 2nd Avenue

S.O.B.'S
www.sobs.com
The Latin beat keeps you dancing at this tropically themed nightclub, Sounds of Brazil. African, reggae and other island music.
🔴 D18 ✉ 200 Varick Street ☎ 212/243-4940 Ⓜ 1 Houston Street

Restaurants

CIVETTA ($$)

You can forgive yourself for feeling that you are dining in Mama's kitchen as Civetta's has a rustic Italian farmhouse feel. A venture from husband and wife chefs, Ron and Colleen Suhanosky, the Mediterranean menu is mainly influenced by Italian cuisine with a touch of Spain, Greece and North Africa.

✚ F18 ⊠ 98 Kenmare Street, between Mulberry and Mott streets ☎ 212/274-9898 ⊠ 6 Spring Street/J, Z Bowery

DELICATESSEN ($)

In need of some comfort food? Then head for Delicatessen where they are served with a twist in a funky SoHo restaurant. Start with Grandma's meatloaf then polish off with milk and cookies.

✚ D18 ⊠ 54 Prince Street ☎ 212/226-0211 ⊠ N, R Prince Street

DOUBLE CROWN ($–$$)

The British Empire meets its former colonies in this original presentation of colonial food from South East Asia and India. A shabby, chic restaurant with overtones of Asia, switch between the Orient and Britain as you start with rice noodles and follow with bangers and mash.

✚ F17 ⊠ 316 Bowery/Bleecker ☎ 212/254-0350 ◷ Closed lunch Mon–Fri ⊠ 6 Bleecker Street/F, M Second Avenue

KATZ'S DELI ($)

www.katzdeli.com

The site of the hilarious climactic scene in *When Harry Met Sally* is the last remaining deli in what was a thriving Jewish neighborhood. Opened in 1888, it upholds traditions: nondescript surroundings and knishes and pastrami sandwiches.

✚ G17 ⊠ 205 E Houston Street/Ludlow Street ☎ 212/254-2246 ⊠ F, M Lower East Side-2nd Avenue

ODEON ($$)

After celebrating its quarter-century in 2005 with all the 80s faces that made it the first hot spot of the *Bright Lights Big City* age, this art deco-style restaurant still outdoes half the new boîtes in town. Its tiled floors, dim lighting, happy bar area and open-most-hours welcome are some reasons why—that and the always-reliable nouvelle-American cooking.

⊠ D20 ⊠ 145 West Broadway/Thomas Street ☎ 212/233-0507 ⊠ A, C Chambers Street

NOBU ($$$)

www.noburestaurants.com

It is difficult to get a reservation at this Japanese shrine, part owned by Robert de Niro, but you'll be rewarded by the hauntingly delicious food. The dining room is a modern Japanese fantasy with lots of bamboo. Choose from sea urchin tempura or fresh yellowtail sashimi with jalapeno.

✚ D19 ⊠ 105 Hudson Street/Franklin Street ☎ 212/219-0500 ◷ Closed Sat, Sun lunch ⊠ 1 Franklin Street

SCHILLERS ($–$$)

www.schillersny.com

The latest hit from the man who brought faux-France to Manhattan (Balthazar, Pastis) veers toward the Mitteleuropa-deli model. It's quite a scene, though off-hours tend to be peaceful.

✚ G18 ⊠ 131 Rivington Street/Norfolk Street ☎ 212/260-4555 ⊠ F, M Delancey Street-2nd Avenue

THOR ($$$)

The name is an acronym for the high-design hotel that houses it. The fabulous Marcel Wanders design is complemented by a soaring glass ceiling that shows off the historic tenement buildings of the Lower East Side. Try the Long Island duck breast with roasted chestnuts.

✚ G18 ⊠ The Hotel on Rivington, 107 Rivington Street/Essex Street ☎ 212/475-2600 ⊠ F Delancey

Downtown

Below 14th Street find the East Village and SoHo where everything from high-fashion stores and ethnic restaurants to bohemian bars and bijou theaters are open (almost) all hours.

Sights	38–43
Walk	44
Shopping	45
Entertainment and Nightlife	46
Restaurants	48

Top 25	25
East Village ▷ 38	
Greenwich Village ▷ 40	
Union Square ▷ 41	

East Village

● Sidewalk artists and book stalls
● Polish-Ukrainian restaurant, Veselka (▷ 48)

● For a calm break, head to Tompkins Square Park, bordered by avenues A and B, between 7th and 10th streets. Once the very definition of "needle park," it couldn't be nicer now, with fresh plantings and children frolicking on the lawns.

Once for those priced out of Greenwich Village, East Village is now expensive bohemia and what used to be the edgiest "nabe" in town is now a youthful playground of restaurants and boutiques with a smattering of historic sights.

Early days The area was settled by Dutch, Irish, German, Jewish and Ukrainian immigrants between 1800 and 1900. By 1830, the Vanderbilt, Astor and Delano families were among those who lived in grand houses on Lafayette Street.

Notable buildings Cooper Union, founded by engineer Peter Cooper and built by 1859, is a designated landmark and it was here that Abraham Lincoln made his famous anti-slavery

Clockwise from top left: typical East Village buildings; two carved lions at the entrance to the church of St. Marks in the Bowery; a colorful delivery vehicle; Astor Place; walking the streets; a decorated building

speech. West of St Mark's Square is the Gothic Revival Grace Church, built in 1846 by James Renwick Jr. Renwick was also responsible for the Federal-style Stuyvesant-Fish House, built in 1803 for Peter Stuyvesant who gave it as a wedding present to his daughter and Nicholas Fish. The Ukrainian Museum is an introduction to the cultural heritage of the Ukrainians who settled here. The displays include decorated Easter eggs, ritual cloths, costumes and a lot more.

Literary appeal A haunt of the Beat poets in the 1960s, East Village attracted Allen Ginsberg, Andy Warhol, Timothy Leary and many radicals. Today the area has its artists and literary types, as well as holding a great appeal to visitors. The range of budget ethnic restaurants and smart eateries offers plenty of choice for lunch.

THE BASICS

✚ F16; east of Bowery and south of 14th Street
🚇 F, M Lower East Side-2nd Avenue; 6 Astor Place

Ukrainian Museum
www.ukrainianmuseum.org
✚ F17
✉ 222 E 6th Street/2nd–3rd avenues
☎ 212/228-0110
🕐 Wed–Sun 11.30–5
💲 Moderate

Greenwich Village

The Row (left); Washington Arch (middle); Jefferson Market Library (right)

THE BASICS

➕ C17

✉ East–west from Broadway to Hudson Street; north–south from 14th Street to Houston Street

🍴 Numerous

🚇 A, B, C, D, E, F 4th Street-Washington Square; 1 Christopher Street-Sheridan Square

🚌 M10

🚆 PATH Christopher Street

♿ Poor

HIGHLIGHTS

● Cafés and jazz clubs
● Washington Square Park
● NYC's narrowest house (75 Bedford Street)
● West (of Hudson Street) Village
● Halloween Parade
● Jefferson Market Library
● Citarella and Jefferson Market (food stores)
● Minetta Lane

This sugar-sweet, picturesque, human-scale neighborhood of brownstones and trees is one of the romantic images of Manhattan, familiar from sitcoms and movies. Its dense streets are rewarding to wander and you can take a break in a café or jazz club.

What village? It was named after Greenwich, southeast London, by the British colonists who settled here at the end of the 17th century. In the 18th and early 19th centuries the wealthy founders of New York society took refuge here from smallpox, cholera and yellow fever.

Bohemia, academe, jazz When the elite moved on, the bohemian invasion began, pioneered by Edgar Allan Poe, who moved to 85 W 3rd Street in 1845. Fellow literary habitués included Mark Twain, O. Henry, Walt Whitman, F. Scott Fitzgerald and Eugene O'Neill. New York University arrived in Washington Square in 1831. Post World War II, bohemia became beatnik; a group of abstract artists, centered around Jackson Pollock, Mark Rothko and Willem de Kooning, also found a home here.

Freedom parades When police raided the Stonewall Inn on June 28, 1969, and arrested gay men for illegally buying drinks, they set off the Stonewall Riots—the birth of the Gay Rights movement. The Inn was on Christopher Street, which became the main drag (no pun intended) of New York's gay community.

For proof that New York is always
evolving, see Union Square. A "needle
park" in the 1970s, it's now where
downtown and uptown meet, with great
restaurants, a wild café scene and the
city's biggest and best Greenmarket.

Not those Unions Laid out in 1839, Union
Square had close encounters with socialism
though its name actually refers to the union of
Broadway and 4th Avenue. It was a mecca for
soapbox orators in the first three decades of the
20th century, then, during the 1930 Depression,
35,000 unemployed rallied here en route to City
Hall to demand work; workers' May Day celebrations convened here, too. Later, Andy Warhol
picked up the vibes, set up his factory, and began
publishing his style mag, *Interview*, where once
the *Daily Worker* had been produced.

Green In summer, the park teems with office
refugees, sharing the lawn with an equestrian
George Washington by John Quincy Adams Ward,
an Abe Lincoln by Henry Kirke Brown and a
Marquis de Lafayette, which Frédéric-Auguste
Bartholdi (of Statue of Liberty fame) gave the city
in 1876. Monday, Wednesday, Friday and Saturday
are Greenmarket days. An entire culture has
grown around this collation of stalls overflowing
with homegrown and homemade produce from
New England farmers, fishers, bakers and growers.
Cult highlights include maple candies, Amish
cheeses, the Pretzel Man (and his pretzels), fresh
clams and local honey from rooftop beehives.

THE BASICS

✚ E15
✉ E 14th–17th streets, Park
Avenue South, Broadway
🕐 Greenmarket Mon,
Wed, Fri, Sat 8–6
🍴 Numerous
🚇 4, 5, 6, L, N, Q, R 14th
Street-Union Square
🚌 M3
♿ Poor

HIGHLIGHTS

● Saturday Greenmarket
● Union Square Café
● Jazz at Blue Water Grill
● Amish Farms stall
● Pretzel Man
● Toys R Us and Virgin
Megastore
● American Savings Bank
building
● Rooftop honey stall
● Apple season
● Terrific branch of Barnes
& Noble

DOWNTOWN

TOP 25

More to See

BLOCK BEAUTIFUL

This picturesque, tree-lined 1920s row really is called this. Also see the pretty square nearby, centered on private Gramercy Park (see opposite page).
☩ E15 ✉ E 19th Street/Irving Place–3rd Avenue Ⓜ N, R 14th Street-Union Square; 6 23rd Street

CHELSEA ART GALLERIES

The main art district is way west. ☩ B14
● **Andrea Rosen** ✉ 525 W 24th Street
☎ 212/627-6000
● **Cheim & Read** ✉ 547 W 25th Street
☎ 212/242-7727
● **Chelsea Art Museum** ✉ 556 W 22nd Street ☎ 212/255-0719
● **Gagosian** ✉ 555 W 24th Street
☎ 212/741-1111
● **Greene Naftali** ✉ 508 W 26th Street, 8th floor ☎ 212/463-7770
● **Marianne Boesky** ✉ 509 W 24th Street ☎ 212/680-9889
● **Mary Boone** ✉ 541 W 24th Street
☎ 212/752-2929
● **Matthew Marks** ✉ 523 W 24th Street
☎ 212/243-0200
● **Max Protech** ✉ 511 W 22nd Street
☎ 212/633-6999
● **Paula Cooper** ✉ 534 W 21st Street
☎ 212/255-1105
● **Sean Kelly** ✉ 528 W 29th Street
☎ 212/239-1181
● **Sonnabend** ✉ 536 W 22nd Street
☎ 212/627-1018
● **Tony Shafrazi** ✉ 544 W 26th Street
☎ 212/274-9300
● **White Box** ✉ 329 Broom Street
☎ 212/714-2347

FLATIRON BUILDING

This 1902 skyscraper was named after its amazing shape: an isosceles triangle with a sharp angle pointing uptown. This instantly recognizable and memorable landmark was designed by Daniel Burnham in 1902.
☩ E14 ✉ 175 5th Avenue/E 22nd–23rd streets Ⓜ N, R 23rd Street

GRACE CHURCH

An outstanding James Renwick-designed Gothic Revival church of the first half of the 19th century. The stained glass is superb, as is the mosaic floor. The original steeple,

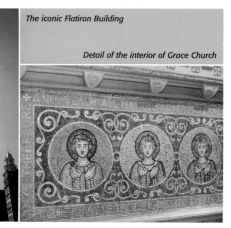

The iconic Flatiron Building

Detail of the interior of Grace Church

constructed in wood, was replaced by a marble one in 1888.

✚ E16 ✉ 802 Broadway ☎ 212/254-2000 🕐 Mon–Fri 10–4, Sun services 🚇 N, R 8th Street-NYU; 6 Astor Place

GRAMERCY PARK HISTORICAL DISTRICT

Peaceful and pleasant to stroll in, Gramercy is centered on the eponymous park. The park is private, locked to all but the residents of the surrounding square. The elegant National Arts Club (15 Gramercy Park South/ 20th Street, tel 212/475-3424) has frequent events open to non-members.

✚ E15 🚇 N, R, 6 23rd Street

MEATPACKING DISTRICT

www.meatpacking-district.com

Bordered roughly by Jane and W 13th streets and 9th Avenue/Greenwich Street, this district was named for its wholesale meat warehouses. Then, around the millennium, the area got so hip so fast, it quickly became not hip at all. But its tangle of boutiques, bars, clubs and restaurants is still something

of a magnet for young New Yorkers.

✚ C16 🚇 A, C, E, L 14th Street

ST. MARKS-IN-THE-BOWERY

The church was built on the site of Peter Stuyvesant's chapel on his farm (*bouwerie*). His grandson sold parcels of the land in today's East Village, and the church purchased the site for the nominal fee of a dollar. Stuyvesant and many of his descendants are buried in the churchyard.

✚ F16 ✉ E 10th Street/2nd Avenue ☎ 212/674-6377 🕐 Events only 🚇 6 Astor Place

WASHINGTON SQUARE: "THE ROW" AND THE ARCH

www.washingtonsquarenyc.org

"The Row" (1–13 north side) housed movers and shakers of 19th-century New York City—read Henry James' *Washington Square*. At the heart of the park is the Arch, designed by Stanford White, where you can watch New Yorkers enjoying themselves.

✚ D17 🚇 N, R 8th Street-NYU; A, B, C, D, E, F, M 4th Street-Washington Square

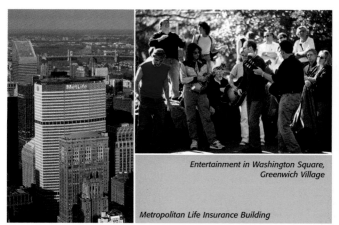

Entertainment in Washington Square, Greenwich Village

Metropolitan Life Insurance Building

Greenwich Village

Architecture, history and quirky shops, plus a visit to the irresistible cupcakes of the Magnolia Bakery.

DISTANCE: 1.5 miles (2.5km) **ALLOW:** 35 minutes

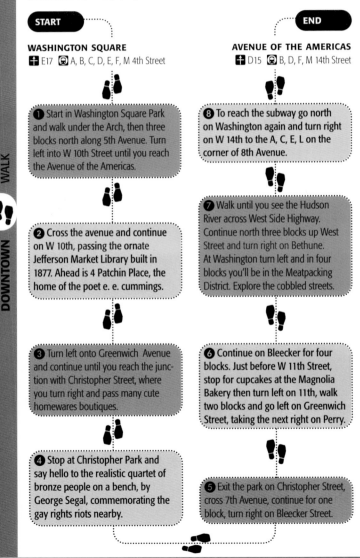

START

WASHINGTON SQUARE
✚ E17 🚇 A, B, C, D, E, F, M 4th Street

END

AVENUE OF THE AMERICAS
✚ D15 🚇 B, D, F, M 14th Street

1 Start in Washington Square Park and walk under the Arch, then three blocks north along 5th Avenue. Turn left into W 10th Street until you reach the Avenue of the Americas.

8 To reach the subway go north on Washington again and turn right on W 14th to the A, C, E, L on the corner of 8th Avenue.

2 Cross the avenue and continue on W 10th, passing the ornate Jefferson Market Library built in 1877. Ahead is 4 Patchin Place, the home of the poet e. e. cummings.

7 Walk until you see the Hudson River across West Side Highway. Continue north three blocks up West Street and turn right on Bethune. At Washington turn left and in four blocks you'll be in the Meatpacking District. Explore the cobbled streets.

3 Turn left onto Greenwich Avenue and continue until you reach the junction with Christopher Street, where you turn right and pass many cute homewares boutiques.

6 Continue on Bleecker for four blocks. Just before W 11th Street, stop for cupcakes at the Magnolia Bakery then turn left on 11th, walk two blocks and go left on Greenwich Street, taking the next right on Perry.

4 Stop at Christopher Park and say hello to the realistic quartet of bronze people on a bench, by George Segal, commemorating the gay rights riots nearby.

5 Exit the park on Christopher Street, cross 7th Avenue, continue for one block, turn right on Bleecker Street.

WALK

DOWNTOWN

Shopping

ABC CARPET AND HOME
Here are seven floors of meticulously edited homewares, from four-poster beds to handkerchiefs, which share an esthetic that mixes Victorian brothel, mid-19th-century design museum, Venetian palace and deluxe hotel.
⊞ E15 ✉ 888 Broadway/19th Street ☎ 212/473-3000 🚇 4, 5, 6, N, Q, R 14th Street-Union Square

CHELSEA MARKET
More than a store, this enormous city-block-size building is several villages' worth of food boutiques, bakeries, cafés, coffee shops and delis under one roof. Even if you're not hungry, stroll through for the architect-honed industrial warehouse meets ancient cave atmosphere.
⊞ C15 ✉ 75 9th Avenue/15th Street ☎ 212/243-6005 🚇 A, C, E, L 14th Street

CYNTHIA ROWLEY
Adorable, hip dresses and shoes. Shop here for a night out on the town.
⊞ C16 ✉ 376 Bleecker Street (between Perry and Charles streets) ☎ 212/242-3803 🚇 1 Christopher Street-Sheridan Square

DSW AND FILENE'S
That's "Designer Shoe Warehouse" with Prada, Kate Spade, Via Spiga et al represented. Upstairs is a three-story Filene's where Dolce & Gabanna, Alberta Feretti and Stella McCartney are among the labels with regular off-price off-season items.
⊞ E15 ✉ 4 Union Square South (University Place) ☎ 212/674-2146 🚇 L, N, Q, R, 4, 5, 6 Union Square

GREENMARKET
Farmers travel from the tri-state area to this outdoor farmers' market that has rejuvenated the entire Union Square area.
⊞ D15–E15 🚇 Mon, Wed, Fri, Sat 8–6 🚇 4, 5, 6, N, R, L Union Square

HOTOVELI
Chic French and Italian creations dominate in this West Village emporium, which caters for the style-conscious ladies and men about town.
⊞ C16 ✉ 271 W 4th Street, between Perry and W 11th streets ☎ 212/206-7722

🚇 1 Christopher Street/Sheridan Square

JEFFREY NEW YORK
The coolest thing in the Meatpacking District, this compact department store of fashion is so high it has vertigo. A resident DJ, a spacious all-white interior and nonpushy assistants make for a pleasant visit—and an expensive one if you fall for the wares.
⊞ B15 ✉ 449 W 14th Street/Washington Street ☎ 212/206-3928 🚇 A, C, E, L 14th Street

LOEHMANN'S
Top designer fashions and labels at hugely reduced prices. Check out the Back Room on the 5th floor. There's another branch on the Upper West Side (Broadway at 73rd Street).
⊞ D15 ✉ 101 7th Avenue/17th Street ☎ 212/352-0856 🚇 1 18th Street

MARC JACOBS
Fashion's favorite darling put once-Bohemian Bleecker Street on the map.
⊞ C16 ✉ 1385, 403, 405 Bleecker Street ☎ 212/924-0026 🚇 1, 2 Christopher Street-Sheridan Square

SCOOP
Hip labels from Daryl K to Tocca and Katayone Adeli, plus cult items like James Perse T's.
⊞ B15 ✉ 430 W 14th Street/Washington Street ☎ 212/691-1905 🚇 A, C, E 14th Street

DOWNTOWN

SHOPPING

Ententainment and Nightlife

APT

www.aptnyc.com
Part club, part music venue, part apartment, this hidden swanky lounge hosts some wild nights.
➕ C16 ✉ 419 W 13th Street/9th Avenue ☎ 212/414-4245 Ⓜ A, C, E 14th Street

BLUE NOTE

www.bluenote.net
Jazz artists from around the world play two shows nightly at this Village jazz club and restaurant.
➕ D17 ✉ 131 W 3rd Street/6th Avenue–MacDougal Street ☎ 212/475-8592 Ⓜ A, C, E, B, D, F 4th Street-Washington Square

CAFÉ WHA?

www.cafewha.com
Since the 1950s this has been a hot spot ever since Bob Dylan and Jimi Hendrix used to hang out here and The Boss started his career here. Bands perform nightly.
➕ D17 ✉ 115 Macdougal/Bleecker-W 3rd Street ☎ 212/254-3706 Ⓜ A, B, C, D, E, F, M 4th St/Washington Square

DUPLEX

www.theduplex.com
Drag queens and downtown crooners sit around the piano bar and have a great time.
➕ D17 ✉ 61 Christopher Street/7th Avenue ☎ 212/255-5438 Ⓜ 1 Christopher Street

GOTHAM COMEDY CLUB

www.gothamcomedyclub.com
Venue for up-and-coming comedians as well as top performers.
➕ C14 ✉ 208 W 23rd Street/7th Avenue ☎ 212/367-9000 Ⓜ N, R, I 23rd Street; F, Path 23rd Street

JOE'S PUB

www.joespub.com
The red velvet bar and performance space named after Joseph Papp, founder of the theater that houses it, has an interesting line-up of singers, comedians, magicians and new wave burlesque artistes.
➕ E16 ✉ The Public Theater, 425 Lafayette Street/Astor Place ☎ 212/967-7555 Ⓜ N, R 8th Street-NYU; 6 Astor Place

MERCURY LOUNGE

www.mercuryloungenyc.com
A laid-back atmosphere that suits eclectic performers. Very few seats.

CABARET

The term has undergone so many image-overhauls, it's now settled into being a catch-all for entertainment options ranging from women-only male burlesque shows (Times Square Hunks, Friday and Saturday nights at Duvet, 45 W 21st Street, 212/989-2121) to drag queen lip-synching and, in the case of Lips (2 Bank Street, 212/675-7710), Bitchy Bingo. Joe's Pub (above) is among the venues that offer what you might call classic, though modernized, cabaret.

➕ F17 ✉ 217 E Houston Street/Avenue A ☎ 212/260-4700 Ⓜ F 2nd Avenue

PETE'S TAVERN

This 1864 Gramercy Park Victorian saloon is where O. Henry wrote *The Gift of the Magi*. No matter how hokey its history, it remains a favorite, thanks to its welcoming feel.
➕ E15 ✉ 129 E 18th Street/Irving Place ☎ 212/473-7676 Ⓜ L, N, R, 4, 6 14th Street-Union Square

PS 122

www.ps122.org
A converted public school that hosts a range of acts from bizarre to poignant.
➕ F16 ✉ 150 1st Avenue/E 9th Street ☎ 212/477-5829 Ⓜ N, R 8th Street; F 2nd Avenue

SING SING KARAOKE

www.karaokesingsing.com
Sing your heart out in this popular karaoke venue that regularly updates its song list.
➕ G17 ✉ 81 Avenue A/E 5th and 6th Street ☎ 212/674-0700 Ⓜ F, M Lower East Side/2nd Avenue

VINTAGE IRVING

www.vintageirving.com
Exposed brick and wood furniture give a European feel. Imbibe fine wines and cocktails and don't leave without trying a sangria or *pinot noir* flavored Wine Cellar Sorbet.
➕ E15 ✉ 118 E 15th Street/Irving Place ☎ 212/677-6300 Ⓜ L 3rd Avenue

Restaurants

PRICES

Prices are approximate, based on a 3-course meal for one person.

$$$	over $60
$$	$40–$60
$	under $40

ALMOND ($$)

www.almondnyc.com
Buzzing American bistro using the freshest ingredients from farm to table; reservations are essential. A warm friendly space often knee-deep with a trendy crowd. The sea scallops are not to be missed and it seems a shame to have to share the mouthwatering apple cinnamon crisp for two.

⊞ E14 ⊠ 12 E 22nd Street/Broadway-Park Avenue ☎ 212/228-7557 ⓠ R 23rd Street

DEL POSTO ($$$)

www.delposta.com
Mario Batali is New York's rotundly ebullient TV-friendly patron saint of interesting Italian food, known for rustic dishes and casual ambience. In his latest concept, he changed the rules: This is a swanky, deco-looking, grown-up, big-night-out grand restaurant, with piano player, theatrical tableside preparations and valet parking. Of course, it works beautifully.

⊞ B15 ⊠ 85 10th Avenue/16th Street ☎ 212/497-8090 ⓠ A, C, E, L 14th Street

GOTHAM BAR AND GRILL ($$$)

www.gothambarandgrill.com
This restaurant epitomizes New York grandeur, with world-class dishes like wild striped bass with haricots verts. The soaring space is light and airy with modern chandeliers.

⊞ E16 ⊠ 12 E 12th Street/5th Avenue ☎ 212/620-4020 ⓞ Closed Sat, Sun lunch ⓠ L, N, R, Q, 4, 5, 6 14th Street/Union Square

GRAMERCY TAVERN ($$–$$$)

www.gramercytavern.com
Gramercy is laid-back, especially if you eat in the less expensive no-reservations area in front, where the food is more rustic. Michael Anthony uses only the freshest market produce in his hearty, utterly reliable new-American food.

⊞ E15 ⊠ 42 E 20th Street/

GIANT SUSHI

For the sushi connoisseur, Yama ($) may not offer the best there is, but it does serve the biggest sushi and it is good. Sadly, many people share this view, and the tiny place is engulfed with salivating sushi wolves, lining up.

⊞ D17 ⊠ 38–40 Carmine Street/Bedford Avenue ☎ 212/989-9330 ⓞ Closed Sun ⓠ 1 Houston Street; A, B, C, D, E, F, M 4th Street/Washington Square

Broadway–Park avenues ☎ 212/477-0777 ⓞ Closed Sat, Sun lunch ⓠ 6, N, R 23rd Street

MARY ANN'S ($)

www.maryannsmexican.com
Homemade Mexican food right down to the fresh tortillas and salsa, with dishes you won't find at your average Tex-Mex. South of the border atmosphere and margaritas by the pint. Cash only.

⊞ C15 ⊠ 116 8th Avenue/16th Street ☎ 212/633-0877 ⓠ C, E 14th Street; L 8th Avenue

THE SPOTTED PIG ($$)

www.spottedpig.com
You're likely to wait an hour or two for a table (you can't reserve) at this Michelin-starred, Anglo-style gastro-pub. Order the gnudi, a kind of ricotta-spinach gnocchi that chef April Bloomfield has made her own.

⊞ D16 ⊠ 314 W 11th Street/Greenwich Avenue ☎ 212/620-0393 ⓠ I, C, E 14th Street; 1 Christopher Street

VESELKA ($)

www.veselka.com
Ukrainian and Polish soul food 24 hours a day. The extensive menu ranges from handmade pierogi to goulash, blintzes to breakfast plates.

⊞ F16 ⊠ 144 2nd Avenue/E 9th Street ☎ 212/228-9682 ⓠ 6 Astor Place; F, M 2nd Avenue; R 8th Street

Definitely a must for visitors to Manhattan, this district has leading museums, a revitalized Times Square, Grand Central Terminal plus the magnet for shoppers—Fifth Avenue with its legendary emporiums.

Sights	52–66	Top 25	**TOP 25**
Walk	67	Chrysler Building ▷ 52	
		Empire State Building ▷ 54	
Shopping	68	Fifth Avenue ▷ 56	
		Grand Central Terminal ▷ 58	
Entertainment	69	Museum of Modern	
and Nightlife		Art ▷ 60	
		New York Public Library ▷ 61	
Restaurants	70	Rockefeller Center ▷ 62	
		Shopping Spree ▷ 63	
		Times Square ▷ 64	

Chrysler Building

HIGHLIGHTS

- Spire
- Ceiling mural
- Elevator cabs
- Setback gargoyles
- African marble lobby

TIP

● From here Grand Central Terminal (▷ 58–59) is no distance at all. Head to the Food Court or Oyster Bar for lunch.

"Which is your favorite New York building?" goes the annoying yet perennial question. Nine out of ten people who express a preference pick the Chrysler Building. This should surprise nobody who gazes on it.

King for a year The tower, commissioned from William Van Alen by Walter Chrysler (who asked for something "taller than the Eiffel Tower"), won the world's tallest building competition in 1930—until the Empire State Building went up the next year. Van Alen had been almost beaten by Craig Severance's Bank of Manhattan tower at 40 Wall Street, when his rival, aware of the unofficial race, slung on an extra two feet. Unknown to Severance, though, Van Alen was constructing a 123ft (37m) stainless-steel spire, which he

The Chrysler Building viewed from the Empire State Building (left); the gleaming lobby (middle); detail of the Chrysler Building's stainless steel spire (below)

"slotted" out through the 925ft (282m) roof, beating the 927-footer hands down. It is ironic that the best view of the art deco beauty's top is from the observatory at the Empire State.

Multistory car Every detail of the 77-story building evokes a 1929 Chrysler Plymouth, to be exact. The winged steel gargoyles are modeled on its radiator caps; the building's stepped setbacks carry stylized hubcaps and the entire spire resembles a radiator grill; and this ain't no Toyota. The golden age of cars is further evoked by the stunning lobby, which you can visit to see the art deco detailing in the red marble, granite and chrome interior, surmounted by the 97ft by 100ft (30m by 31m) mural depicting industrial scenes and celebrating "transportation." Don't miss the marquetry elevator doors.

THE BASICS

✚ E11
✉ 405 Lexington Avenue/ 42nd Street
🕐 Mon–Fri office hours; closed holidays
🚇 4, 5, 6, 7, S Grand Central-42nd Street, Grand Central
🚌 M101, M102, M103, M104
🚆 Metro North, Grand Central
♿ Good
🎟 Free

Empire State Building   TOP 25

HIGHLIGHTS

● The view: by day, at dusk and by night
● The view up from 34th Street
● Observatory Audio Tour
● Lights on the top stories

TIP

● The colored lights at the summit were introduced in 1976 and are changed to mark different events. You can avoid the line (though not the security one) by printing out advance tickets from the website.

It was not Fay Wray's fault, nor Cary Grant's in *An Affair to Remember*, that this is the most famous skyscraper in the world. Rather, its fame is the reason it has appeared in every New York movie. You have to climb this.

King for 40 years This is the very definition of "skyscraper," and it was the highest man-made thing until the late, lamented World Trade Center was built in the 1970s. Now it is once again the tallest building in New York, although this will change when the Freedom Tower is completed (▷ panel, 5). Construction began in 1930, not long before the great Wall Street Crash, and by the time it was topped out in 1931—construction went at the superfast rate of four stories a week—so few could afford to rent space, they called it "the

Clockwise from left: the Empire State Building; the buildings of Midtown look small when viewed from the top; the towering structure soars high into the sky; the observation deck; the lobby

Empty State Building." Only the popularity of its observatories kept the wolves from the door. These viewpoints still attract 3.8 million visitors each year. The 86th floor Observatory, with its glass-enclosed, climate-controlled area, is a highlight, but if you can't make the trip, there is a virtual tour available online.

Facts It is 1,454ft (443m) high, with 103 floors. The frame contains 60,000 tons of steel, 10 million bricks line the building, and there are 6,500 windows. The speediest of the 73 elevators climb about 1000ft (330m) per minute. The fastest runners in the annual Empire State Run-Up climb the 1,860 steps (not open to the public) to the 102nd floor in just over nine minutes. The observation deck on the 102nd floor requires a separate ticket and additional fee, which is purchased on arrival.

THE BASICS

www.esbnyc.com
✚ D13
✉ 350 5th Avenue/
W 34th Street
☎ 212/736-3100
🕐 Daily 8am–2am; last
admission 1.15am
🍽 Restaurants
🚇 B, D, F, N, Q, R 34th
Street-Herald Square
🚌 M10, M16, M34
🚉 PATH 34th Street/
Avenue of the Americas
♿ Good
💲 Expensive

HIGHLIGHTS

- Shopping!
- Empire State Building
- Rockefeller Center
- The Met
- The Guggenheim
- The Cooper-Hewitt

TIP

- Try to see a parade—
St. Patrick's Day Parade, the
biggest, is on March 17.

Think shopping in New York and Fifth Avenue is likely to be your next thought. But there is more here: Museums, smart hotels and landmark buildings rub shoulders with FAO Schwartz, Saks Fifth Avenue and an Apple Store that never shuts.

Tradition and invention Fifth Avenue runs all the way from Washington Square Park up past Central Park and it houses some of the most pricey and notable real estate in New York. Walk along the avenue and you'll pass the Flatiron Building (▷ 42), Empire State Building (▷ 54), the New York Public Library (▷ 61), the Rockefeller Center (▷ 62), the Metropolitan Museum of Art (▷ 80), the Guggenheim (▷ 78), St. Patrick's Cathedral (▷ 66) and the Cooper-Hewitt (▷ 76), just a few of the buildings that represent the development of

Fifth Avenue from a sought-after address lined with mansions to an important artery of this vibrant city.

Shop, shop, shop The shopping venues that favor kids will be the reinvented FAO Schwarz and the Disney Store. Parents might prefer the jewelry emporia of Tiffany & Co. and Cartier, and the famous department stores. Saks Fifth Avenue has been at its Renaissance-style building since 1922. The poshest store of all, Bergdorf Goodman, is at 57th Street, the fashion mecca Henri Bendel is at 56th, and that temple of stylish casual wear, Abercrombie & Fitch, is also at 56th.

Relax Two excellent hotels stand on 55th Street: the Peninsula New York, with great vistas from its Pentop Bar and Terrace Grill, and the St-Regis Hotel with the King Cole Bar.

THE BASICS

➕ D16–D7
✉ From Washington Square to the Harlem River
🚇 4, 5, 6
🚌 M1, M2, M3, M4

Grand Central Terminal

HIGHLIGHTS

- Main Concourse ceiling
- Oyster Bar
- Chandeliers
- Whispering Gallery
- The clock
- The 75ft (23m) arched windows
- Grand Staircase

TIP

● Take the self-guided walking tour starting at the four-sided clock, a world-famous rendezvous spot.

Don't call it a station. All tracks terminate here, which makes this—yes—a terminal. The Beaux-Arts building bustles like no place else. As the saying goes—stand here long enough and the entire world passes by.

Heart of the nation "Grand Central Station!" bellowed (erroneously) the 1937 opening of the eponymous NBC radio drama; "Beneath the glitter and swank of Park Avenue…Crossroads of a million private lives!…Heart of the nation's greatest city…" And so it is, and has been since 1871 when the first, undersize version was opened by Commodore Cornelius Vanderbilt, who had bought up all the city's railroads, just like on a giant Monopoly board. See him in bronze below Jules-Alexis Coutans' allegorical statuary on the

Clockwise from left: the busy main concourse at Grand Central Terminal; the entrance to the terminal; people riding the escalator; detail of the clock

main facade (south, 42nd Street). The current building dates from 1913 and is another Beaux Arts glory, its design modeled partly on the Paris Opéra by architects Warren and Wetmore. William Wilgus was the logician responsible for traffic-marshaling, while Reed & Stem were the overall engineers. Look up at the main concourse ceiling for the stunning sight of 2,500 "stars" in a cerulean sky, with medieval-style zodiac signs by French artist Paul Helleu.

Look within The fame of the four-faced clock atop the information booth is out of proportion to its size. Below ground is a warren of 32 miles (52km) of tracks, tunnels and vaulted chambers; in one the famed Oyster Bar resides. The Food Court is virtually a new neighborhood. Be careful what you say here—the acoustics are amazing.

THE BASICS

www.grandcentralterminal.com

☩ E11

✉ Park Avenue/E 42nd Street

☎ 212/532-4900

🕐 Daily 5.30am–1.30am; Story Booth daily 24 hours

🍴 Restaurant, café/bar, snack bars

🚇 4, 5, 6, 7, S Grand Central-42nd Street

🚌 M1, M2, M3, M4, M5, M42, M98, M101, 102 Grand Central

🚆 Metro North, Grand Central

♿ Good   👋 Free

❓ Tours Wed 12.30pm. Meet by information booth in main concourse

☎ 212/935-3960

Museum of Modern Art

Views of MoMA (left and middle); David and Peggy Rockefeller Building (right)

THE BASICS

www.moma.org
➕ D10
✉ 11 W 53rd Street/
5th–6th avenues
☎ 212/708-9400
🕐 Sat–Mon, Wed, Thu
10.30–5.30, Fri 10.30–8
(Jul–Aug Thu until 8.45)
🍴 Restaurant
🚇 E, M 5th Avenue/53rd
Street; B, D, F 47th–50th
streets-Rockefeller Center
🚌 M1, 2, 3, 4, 5
♿ Good
💲 Expensive; free Fri 4–8

HIGHLIGHTS

● *Hope*, Klimt (1907–08)
● *Dance*, Matisse (1909)
● *Les Demoiselles d'Avignon*, Picasso (1907)
● *Starry Night*, Van Gogh (1889)
● *Gas*, Hopper (1940)
● *One*, Pollock (1950)
● *Flag*, Jasper Johns (1954–55)

Opened in November 2004, the new MoMA building, designed by Japanese architect Yoshio Taniguchi, has been called a work of art, and at 630,000sq ft (58,527sq m) it has nearly twice the capacity of the old museum.

Van Gogh to Man Ray Founded on the 1931 bequest of Lillie P. Bliss, which consisted of 235 works, the collections now amount to about 150,000 pieces. These include household objects, photography, graphic design, conceptual art, media and industrial design.

Postimpressionists to graffiti artists The collection starts in the late 19th century, with the Postimpressionists and Fauvists. Among the 20th-century movements represented are Cubism, Futurism, Expressionism, Surrealism, Abstract Expressionism, Pop (Oldenburg, Dine, Rauschenberg and Warhol) and the "Graffiti" work of Keith Haring and Jean-Michel Basquiat.

Even more modern A sunlighted 110ft (33m) high atrium affording a view of the beloved Abby Aldrich Rockefeller Sculpture Garden heralds the all-new MoMA, featuring much use of glass, granite, aluminum and floods of light. Taniguchi designed individual galleries specifically for the media they house, including new ones for contemporary art and new media. Restaurants operated by restaurateur Danny Meyer raise the glamour quotient, that is, if this modern art collection didn't already do so.

QUIET ZONE

MIDTOWN ★ TOP 25

Why are we sending you to a library on your vacation? Because the New York Public Library's Central Research Building is a great, white, hushed palace, beautiful to behold even if you have no time to open a book.

The building Carrère and Hastings (who also designed the Frick, ▷ 77) were the architects of what is generally thought the city's best representative of the Beaux Arts style—the sumptuous yet classical French school that flourished from 1880 to 1920 in New York. A pair of lions, which Mayor LaGuardia christened Patience and Fortitude, flank the majestic stair that leads directly into the vaulted, carved white marble temple of Astor Hall. The lions are themselves flanked by fountains, "Truth" and "Beauty." Behind this briefly stood New York's version of London's Crystal Palace, built for the first American World's Fair in 1853. Like the London one, it burned down. Inside, see temporary exhibitions in the Gottesman Hall, and look up! The carved oak ceiling is sublime; read in the two-block-long Main Reading Room; see library collection rarities in the Salomon Room; and don't miss the Richard Haas murals of NYC publishing houses in the De Witt Wallace Periodical Room.

The books The library owns more than 15 million books, most living in the 82 branches. This building is dedicated to research. The CATNYP computer can disgorge any of the 16 million manuscripts or 3 million books from the 92 miles (148km) of stacks in 10 minutes flat.

THE BASICS

www.nypl.org
🔲 D11
✉ 476 5th Avenue/42nd Street
☎ 212/930-0800
🕐 Mon, Thu–Sat 10–6; Tue–Wed 10–9, Sun 1–5; closed holidays
🍴 Kiosks outside (summer)
🚇 4, 5, 6, S Grand Central-42nd Street, 7 5th Avenue
🚌 M1, M2, M3, M4, M5, M6, M7, M42, M104
🚆 Metro North, Grand Central
♿ Good
🖐 Free

HIGHLIGHTS

● Patience and Fortitude
● "Truth" and "Beauty"
● T. S. Eliot's typescript of *The Waste Land*
● Jefferson's handwritten Declaration of Independence
● Astor Hall
● American Jewish Oral History Collection
● Gottesman Hall ceiling

Rockefeller Center

People outside the center (left); Prometheus statue (middle) beside the ice rink (right)

THE BASICS

www.rockefellercenter.com

D10

5th–6th Avenues/ 48th–51st streets

212/632-3975

Various

Many restaurants, cafés

B, D, F, M 47th–50th streets-Rockefeller Center

M1, M2, M3, M4, M5, M27, M50

Moderate Free

Radio City tours 212/ 307-7171; NBC Studio tours 212/664-3700; Rockefeller Center tours 212/698-2000

Top of the Rock

www.topoftherocknyc.com

212/698-2000

Daily 8am–midnight (last shuttle 11pm)

Expensive

HIGHLIGHTS

● Top of the Rock Observation Deck
● GE Building's lobbies
● NBC Studio tour
● Skating in winter
● Radio City Music Hall
● *Prometheus* (1934)
● *Atlas* (5th Avenue, 50th–51st streets)

This small village of famous art deco buildings provides many of those "Gee, this is New York" moments, especially in winter when you see ice-skaters ringed by the flags of the UN and gaze up at the massive tree.

Prometheus is here The 19-building Rockefeller Center has been called "the greatest urban complex of the 20th century." John D. Rockefeller Jr.'s grand real estate scheme provided work for a quarter of a million souls during the Depression. Its centerpiece is the elongated ziggurat GE Building (formerly the RCA building) at 30 Rockefeller Plaza, adorned with Lee Lawrie's glass-and-limestone frieze, lobby murals by José Maria Sert and other artworks. Rest on a Channel Gardens bench and gaze on the lower plaza, the rink and Paul Manship's *Prometheus*.

Top of the Rock The three-tiered observation deck at the top of the GE building affords stunning panoramic views over Manhattan and the only such public view over Central Park. The mezzanine museum gives historical highlights of the complex before high-speed elevators whisk you to the 67th–70th floor viewing platforms at the very top.

SNL and Rockettes The GE Building also houses NBC Studios. Take a studio tour or join the line for standby tickets to the popular show "Saturday Night Live." Over on Avenue of the Americas is Radio City Music Hall, which is the landmark home to the Rockettes.

A restrained display window (left); shoppers thronging Fifth Avenue (right)

Shopping Spree

What is great about shopping in New York is the way you come across cool stores all over the place, and also the sheer quantity of shopping neighborhoods. Here is an easy two-part shopping mission that you can manage (just about) in one day.

SoHo crawl Start with a coffee and pastry at Dean and DeLuca (Broadway/Prince). You're opposite the museumlike Prada store with Kate's Paperie (▷ 32) two blocks away. Huge H&M and Zara stores are also here. Head south down Broadway for Scoop (▷ 45) and branches of the underwear queen, Victoria's Secret (at Spring) and the cosmetics sweet shop Sephora (555 Broadway); Banana Republic (women at 552, men at 528) and Old Navy; you'll also see shoe stores carrying sneakers and casual brands like Frye, Dansko and Merrill (for fabulous fashion shoes go one block east to Otto Tootsi Plohound at 273 Lafayette Street). On the east side of the street is the downtown branch of Bloomingdale's (504 Broadway). Now head down Broome, stopping at Gourmet Garage (▷ 32) for a snack, check out Kate Spade accessories opposite and head north on Mercer, Greene or Wooster. Here you're on your own, with lots of stores to explore.

Madison Avenue The next leg is easier. Take the F from Broadway-Lafayette Street to Lexington Avenue/63rd Street, walk west across Park Avenue to Madison Avenue and turn left. Head straight to Barneys (▷ 85), then work your way slowly down. Well done!

THE BASICS

SoHo Crawl
🚇 N, R Prince Street

Madison Avenue
🚇 F Lexington Avenue/63rd Street

HIGHLIGHTS

● Areas not covered here include (but are not restricted to) Herald Square (Macy's and huge branches of H&M, Old Navy, Gap, Victoria's Secret); Fifth Avenue (▷ 56–57); the *other* Fifth Avenue in Park Slope, plus other Brooklyn strips at Smith Street (Boerum Hill/Carroll Gardens) and Bedford Avenue (Williamsburg) all teeming with enchanting independent boutiques. Then there's Nolita, the grid of dinky high-fashion stores centered on Elizabeth Street; the multiple hipster emporia of the Lower East Side and the "big box" stores of Chelsea.

Times Square

Stretch limo in Times Square (left); looking up from Times Square (right)

THE BASICS

www.timessquarenyc.org

C11

Times Square Visitors Center ✉ 1560 Broadway/ 7th Avenue

☎ 212/869-1890

Ⓜ 1, 2, 3, 7, N, Q, R, S Times Square-42nd Street

🕐 8–8

❓ Free "Times Square Exposé" tour, Friday at noon

HIGHLIGHTS

● New Victory Theater
● Shubert Alley
● Toys R Us indoor Ferris wheel
● ABC's *Good Morning* studio: 44th/Broadway
● Live appearances at MTC TRL studio
● New Year's Eve ball drop

TIP

● The cash-only TKTS booth, temporarily located at the Marriott Marquis Hotel at 46th Street between Broadway and 8th Avenue, is good for same-day theater tickets for 20–50 percent off. It's open daily 3–8pm for evening shows; Wednesday and Saturday 10–2, Sunday 3–half hour before last curtain time.

"The Crossroads of the World," one-time symbol of Manhattan glitz and glam, is an area New Yorkers love to hate—especially since it has been sanitized. You may disagree as you explore the big stores and get dazzled by the neon.

Longacre The junction of Broadway and 7th Avenue wasn't even called Times Square until 1904. It was "The Longacre" until Times Tower, the new home of the *New York Times*, was finished. Almost immediately, the invention of neon light, the opening of the first subway line and the decision to site the city's New Year celebration here conspired to make the triangular square the de facto center of Manhattan.

On Broadway The theaters moved in and Broadway, the Great White Way, became synonymous with bigtime showbiz: popular theatrical—especially musical—division. By 1914 there were 43 theaters in the immediate vicinity; after multiple closings, refurbishments and reopenings, there are some 22 of them today.

Best of Times, Worst of Times By the 1970s Times Square was one of the most crime-ridden neighborhoods in the city, rife with porn emporia of all kinds, drug-dealing and assorted vileness. The dawn of the 1990s saw the rebirth with several city-run and independent organizations working to clean up and reglamorize. As the giant stores, state-of-the-art illuminations and even the Armed Forces recruiting station show, it worked.

INTERNATIONAL CENTER OF PHOTOGRAPHY

www.icp.org

In the heart of Midtown, the ICP is both a school and a museum. Temporary exhibitions are always on view, and the permanent collection has 60,000 photographs ranging from old daguerreotypes to iris prints, mainly from American and European reportage and documentation from the 1930s to the present. There are photographs by such well-known names as Henri Cartier-Bresson, Elliott Erwitt and Harold Edgerton, along with a collection of 13,000 original prints by Weegee, who photographed crime scenes and New York nightlife in the 1930s and 1940s.

🚩 D11 ✉ 1133 Avenue of the Americas/43rd Street ☎ 212/857-0000 🕐 Tue–Thu 10–6, Fri 10–8, Sat–Sun 10–6 🚇 B, D, F, M 42nd Street 👋 Expensive

"LIPSTICK BUILDING"

This likeable 1986 show-off is by John Burgee with Philip Johnson.

🚩 F10 ✉ 885 3rd Avenue/54th Street 🚇 E, M Lexington Avenue

MADISON SQUARE GARDEN

www.thegarden.com

Above Penn Station, a venue for concerts, sports events and the home of the New York Knicks basketball team.

🚩 C13 ✉ 4 Penn Plaza ☎ 212/465-6741 🚇 A, C, E, 1, 2, 3, 34th Street-Penn Station

MORGAN LIBRARY & MUSEUM

www.themorgan.org

The Renzo Piano extension has doubled the library's gallery space and added a new Reading Room and Madison Avenue entrance. The collection was started by financier John Pierpont Morgan at the end of the 19th century. It includes the 9th-century Lindau Gospels, a rare vellum copy of the Gutenberg Bible, the medieval Dutch masterpiece *The Hours of Catherine of Cleves*, scores by Beethoven, Mozart and Puccini and manuscripts by authors Jane Austen, Charles Dickens and Mark Twain.

🚩 E12 ✉ 225 Madison Avenue/E 36th Street ☎ 212/685-0008 🕐 Tue–Thu 10.30–5, Fri 10.30–9, Sat 10–6, Sun 11–6 🚇 4, 5, 6 33rd Street 👋 Expensive

Inside the International Center of Photography

PALEY CENTER FOR MEDIA

www.paleycenter.org

The museum was established in 1989 on land donated by William S. Paley, a former chairman of broadcasting giant CBS. The archive of 100,000 tapes of programs and commercials span nearly 100 years. When you arrive, make a reservation to use the computer catalog on the fourth floor to locate what interests you, then reserve it and watch it in one of the museum's consoles. Or you can take in a show or two at one of the screening rooms or theaters. Seminars and classes, as well as exhibitions, are held throughout the year.

➕ D10 ✉ 25 W 52nd Street ☎ 212/621-6800 🕓 Wed–Sun 12–6, Thu until 8, Fri theater programs 🚇 E, M 5th Avenue/53rd Street 🚻 Moderate

ST. PATRICK'S CATHEDRAL

www.stpatrickscathedral.org

James Renwick's Gothic Revival cathedral is the US's biggest for Roman Catholics, seating around 2,200. The beautiful St. Michael and St. Louis altar was designed by Tiffany & Co.

➕ E10 ✉ 460 Madison Avenue ☎ 212/753-2261 🕓 Services at various times; tours available on request 🚇 6 51st Street; E, M 5th Avenue/53rd Street

TRUMP TOWER

"Glitz" captured in pink marble and glass. The top floors house apartments, while below is a six-floor atrium with shops, waterfalls and greenery.

➕ E9 ✉ 721 5th Avenue/56th Street ☎ 212/832-2000 🕓 Daily 8am–10pm 🍴 Several 🚇 E, N, R, M 5th Avenue

UNITED NATIONS HEADQUARTERS

The 544ft (166m) Secretariat building that dominates the site opened in 1950. Alongside are the General Assembly building, the Conference building (fronting the river) and the Dag Hammarskjöld Library. A guided tour covers the General Assembly Hall and Security Council Chamber.

➕ G11 ✉ United Nations Plaza ☎ 212/963-8687 🕓 Mon–Fri 9.45–4.45 (check in advance) 🍴 Restaurant 🚇 4, 5, 6, 7 Grand Central-42nd Street 🚻 Expensive

St. Patrick's Cathedral

Trump Tower

Midtown Stroll

Madison Square Garden, the Empire State Building, Chrysler Building, Grand Central Station and Fifth Avenue—what more could one want?

DISTANCE: 2 miles (3km) **ALLOW:** 40 minutes (and more for Central Park)

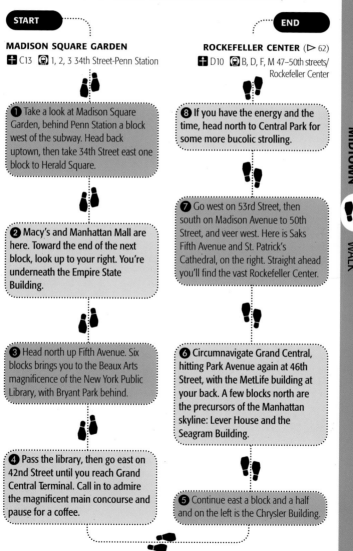

START

MADISON SQUARE GARDEN
C13 1, 2, 3 34th Street-Penn Station

END

ROCKEFELLER CENTER (▷ 62)
D10 B, D, F, M 47–50th streets/
Rockefeller Center

1 Take a look at Madison Square Garden, behind Penn Station a block west of the subway. Head back uptown, then take 34th Street east one block to Herald Square.

8 If you have the energy and the time, head north to Central Park for some more bucolic strolling.

2 Macy's and Manhattan Mall are here. Toward the end of the next block, look up to your right. You're underneath the Empire State Building.

7 Go west on 53rd Street, then south on Madison Avenue to 50th Street, and veer west. Here is Saks Fifth Avenue and St. Patrick's Cathedral, on the right. Straight ahead you'll find the vast Rockefeller Center.

3 Head north up Fifth Avenue. Six blocks brings you to the Beaux Arts magnificence of the New York Public Library, with Bryant Park behind.

6 Circumnavigate Grand Central, hitting Park Avenue again at 46th Street, with the MetLife building at your back. A few blocks north are the precursors of the Manhattan skyline: Lever House and the Seagram Building.

4 Pass the library, then go east on 42nd Street until you reach Grand Central Terminal. Call in to admire the magnificent main concourse and pause for a coffee.

5 Continue east a block and a half and on the left is the Chrysler Building.

MIDTOWN

WALK

Shopping

APPLE STORE

This 24-hour-a-day, 365-day-a-year showcase store is certain to delight the Mac-geeks and trendy young things who fall under the spell of Apple's industry-leading design and stylish simplicity.
⊞ D9 ⊠ 767 5th Avenue at 59th Street ☎ 212/336-1440 Ⓜ N, R to 5th Avenue/59th Street

BERGDORF GOODMAN

For the most sophisticated shopping experience in New York, the eight-floor fashion-for-lunching-ladies department store in the former Vanderbilt mansion takes the cake.
⊞ E9 ⊠ 754 5th Avenue/57th Street ☎ 212/753-7300 Ⓜ N, R 5th Avenue/59th Street

FAO SCHWARZ

The near-legendary toy store has lost its iconic giant clockwork tower but gained a whole new lease of life. There are plenty of areas for kids to experiment with giant toys you have no intention of dragging home. Don't forget to dance on the piano from *Big*.
⊞ E9 ⊠ 767 5th Avenue/58th Street ☎ 212/644-9400 Ⓜ N, R 5th Avenue/59th Street

MACY'S

The sign outside says it's the largest store in the world, and by the time you've made your way across the nine-block-long floors of this grandfather of all department stores, you'll believe them. Everything (including thousands of other shoppers) is here.
⊞ D12 ⊠ 151 W 34th Street-Herald Square ☎ 212/695-4400 Ⓜ B, D, F, N, R 34th Street

MANOLO BLAHNIK

Stunning creations for the feet that are sought after by fashionistas and celebrities alike.
⊞ D10 ⊠ 31 W 54th Street ☎ 212/582-3077 Ⓜ E, M 5th Avenue/53rd Street

MICHAEL C. FINA

Every bride wants her wedding list at this very exclusive purveyor of gifts and tableware.
⊞ E11 ⊠ 545 5th Avenue/45th Street ☎ 212/557-2500 Ⓜ 4, 5, 6, 7 Grand Central

---

COLUMBUS CIRCLE

The closest thing to a mall in Manhattan, this splashy high-rise reclaimed drab Columbus Circle from the traffic when it opened in 2004. Upstairs are posh restaurants, plus the Mandarin Oriental hotel and a swanky health club. The lowest four levels contain the shopping experience. The *pièce de résistance* is the below-ground-level Whole Foods Market (see right)—a Texan-born upscale grocery chain.

NIKE TOWN NY

Feel like a professional athlete here. High-tech videos, multilevel displays and an industrial atmosphere encourage aerobic shopping.
⊞ D9 ⊠ 6 E 57th Street, between 5th and Madison ☎ 212/891-6453 Ⓜ N, R 57th Street

SAKS FIFTH AVENUE

The flagship store of the now nationwide chain, with a fabulous range of designer fashions for men as well as women, and a great beauty department.
⊞ E10 ⊠ 611 5th Avenue/49th–50th streets ☎ 212/753-4000 Ⓜ E, F 5th Avenue

TAKASHIMAYA

An austere Japanese esthetic informs the atmosphere of this small but exquisite department store. Housewares and gifts are the main focus.
⊞ E9 ⊠ 693 5th Avenue/55th Street ☎ 212/350-0100 Ⓜ E, F 5th Avenue

WHOLE FOODS MARKET

The lower floor of the Time Warner Center is by far New York's largest food store. Find prepared food of every kind, hot bars of Indian, Latin and Asian dishes, cafés, baked goods, fish, cheeses, meat, fruit…
⊞ C9 ⊠ Concourse Level, Time Warner Center, Broadway (59th/60th Street) ☎ 212/823-9600 Ⓜ A, B, C, D, 1 59th Street-Columbus Circle

Entertainment and Nightlife

BIRDLAND

www.birdlandjazz.com
Big names, big bands,
Coltrane tributes and
Cubans is the range here.
➕ C11 ✉ 315 W 44th
Street/8th–9th avenues
☎ 212/581-3080 🚇 A, C, E
42nd Street-Port Authority
Bus Terminal

CARNEGIE HALL

www.carnegiehall.org
This world-class recital
hall features an eclectic
program from classical
artists to folk singers.
➕ D9 ✉ 881 7th Avenue/
57th Street ☎ 212/247-7800
🚇 N, R 57th Street; E 7th
Avenue

ETHEL BARRYMORE THEATRE

Opened in 1928, this
theater saw Fred Astaire
perform in the 30s, at the
start of his movie career.
➕ C11 ✉ 243 W 47th Street/
Broadway–8th Avenue
☎ 212/239-6200 🚇 1, C, E
50th Street; N, R 49th Street

FOUR SEASONS HOTEL

www.fourseasons.com
I. M. Pei's design gives
this a sleek, austere
ene-rgy. Impressive
Martini menu.
➕ E9 ✉ 57 E 57th Street/
Madison Avenue ☎ 212/758-
5700 🚇 4, 5, 6 Lexington
Avenue-59th Street

THE LATE SHOW WITH DAVID LETTERMAN

www.cbs.com/late_night
Catch the top-rated US
chat show at one of its
weeknight outings from
a venue in the heart of
theatreland. Letterman
draws A-list names from
the worlds of music, film,
comedy and politics.
➕ C10 ✉ 1697 Broadway
🚇 1 50th Street-Broadway

THE LAURIE BEECHMAN THEATRE

www.beechmantheatre.com
In the basement of the
West Bank Café, this
supper club hosts regular
performances by comedy
legend Joan Rivers.
➕ B11 ✉ 407 W 42nd
Street/9th Avenue
☎ 212/695-6909 🚇 1, 2, 3,
7, N, Q, R Times Square-42nd
Street

MADISON SQUARE GARDEN

www.thegarden.com
The not-so-beautiful giant
concrete circle is one of
the city's major venues
for music and sporting

events. For the box office
enter the Main Ticket
Lobby at 7th Avenue and
32nd Street.
➕ C13 ✉ 4 Pennsylvania
Plaza 🚇 1, 2, 3 34th Street-
Penn Station

THE NEW VICTORY THEATER

www.newvictory.org
If you have kids of any
age (over 5) in tow,
there'll be something
here to thrill them—and,
chances are, you also.
One of the best youth-
centric programs.
➕ C11 ✉ 209 W 42nd
Street/7th–8th avenues
☎ 646/223-3010 🚇 1, 2, 3,
7, N, R, Q Times Square-42nd
Street

NOKIA THEATRE

www.nokiatheatrenyc.com
A medium-size venue for
medium-big acts in the
center of Times Square.
➕ C11/D11 ✉ 1515
Broadway/44th Street
☎ 212/930-1959 🚇 1, 2, 3,
7, N, Q, R, S Times Square-
42nd Street

RADIO CITY MUSIC HALL

www.radiocity.com
This landmark art deco
theater hosts several
music shows a year. You
can take an hour-long
tour and learn all about
its life since it opened
in 1932.
➕ D10 ✉ 1260 6th Avenue/
50th Street ☎ 212/307-7171
🕐 Varied. Tours daily 11–3
🚇 B, D, F, M 40th–50th
streets-Rockefeller Center

MIDTOWN ENTERTAINMENT AND NIGHTLIFE

Restaurants

PRICES

Prices are approximate, based on a 3-course meal for one person.

$$$	over $60
$$	$40–$60
$	under $40

'21' CLUB ($$$)

With a history spanning seven decades, this eatery still nods a cap to its speakeasy days while having a foot firmly in the modern. The burger is a perennial menu favorite.
➕ D10 ✉ 21 W 52nd Street/ 5th–6th avenues ☎ 212/ 582–7200 🕐 Closed Sun 🚇 B, D, F, M 47th–50th streets-Rockefeller Center

LE BERNARDIN ($$$)

www.le-bernardin.com
Frenchman Eric Ripert is acknowledged to be the fish maestro. Exquisite, inventive dishes are served by super-attentive waiters.
➕ D10 ✉ 155 W 51st Street/ 7th Avenue ☎ 212/554-1515 🕐 Closed Sat lunch, Sun 🚇 B, D, F, M 47th–50th streets-Rockefeller Center

CASER LEVER ($$–$$$)

www.casalever.com
The mid-century modern ocean liner-esque design by Mark Newman is the star of this restaurant downstairs at the iconic 1952 building on Park Avenue, but it would be worth visiting for chef Dan Silverman's eclectic-contemporary menu alone.
➕ E10 ✉ 390 Park Avenue/ 53rd Street ☎ 212/888-2700 🚇 E, M Lexington Avenue/ 53rd Street; 6 51st Street

FOUR SEASONS ($$$)

Every once in a while a restaurant defines an age, and then transcends it. The Four Seasons changed the face of New York dining. Choose between the dark wood Grill Room and the romantic Pool Room.
➕ E10 ✉ 99 E 52nd Street/ Park–Lexington avenues ☎ 212/754-9494 🕐 Closed Sat lunch, Sun 🚇 6 51st Street

JOHN'S

www.johnspizzerianyc.com
This converted church has one of just a handful of coal brick-ovens left in the city. It's a great spot for pre- or post-theater, and the pizzas are amazing.
➕ C11 ✉ 260 W 44th Street

TERMINAL FEEDING

Here are some highlights at the Food Court at Grand Central Terminal:
Café Spice for curries.
Caviarteria is as it sounds—fish eggs and champagne.
Custard Beach is all about the richest, bestest vanilla ice cream.
Junior's is a great diner with peerless cheesecake.
Knödel does wurst, boudin, merguez…
Mindy's Kosher Delicatessen does knishes and pastrami-on-rye.

➕ 212/391-7560 🚇 1, 2, 3, 7, N, Q, R Times Square/42nd Street.

THE MODERN ($$$)

With young star chef, Alasatian-born, Gabriel Kreuther behind the range, MoMA's fancy restaurant is not just for museum visits. Expect fascinating takes on modern French food.
➕ D10 ✉ 9 W 53rd Street/5th–6th avenues ☎ 212/333-1220 🕐 Closed Sat lunch, Sun 🚇 E, M 5th Avenue/53rd Street

OYSTER BAR ($$)

www.oysterbar.com
Some reports suggest this 1913 vaulted room in Grand Central Station may be resting on past glories but for a thoroughly New York experience it's pretty hard to beat.
➕ E11 ✉ Grand Central Terminal, lower level ☎ 212/490-6650 🕐 Closed Sun 🚇 4, 5, 6, 7 Grand Central-42nd Street

PER SE ($$$)

www.perseny.com
If you want to know what all the fuss is about, reserve *way* ahead for French Laundry-maestro Thomas Keller's amazing, precise and idiosyncratic food. Try for a table by the window for great views
➕ C9 ✉ Time Warner Center, 10 Columbus Circle, 4th floor/60th Street ☎ 212/823-9335 🕐 Closed Mon–Thu lunch 🚇 A, B, C, D, 1 59th Street-Columbus Circle

GENHEIM

Central Park is the city's lungs—a huge green space for all Manhattan. Visit the zoo; see free summer Shakespeare or bring a picnic. The museums of the Upper East Side are renowned worldwide.

Sights	74–84	Top 25	TOP 25
Shopping	85	Central Park ▷ 74	
		Cooper-Hewitt National Design Museum ▷ 76	
Entertainment and Nightlife	86	Frick Collection ▷ 77	
		Guggenheim Museum ▷ 78	
Restaurants	88	Metropolitan Museum of Art ▷ 80	
		Whitney Museum of American Art ▷ 82	

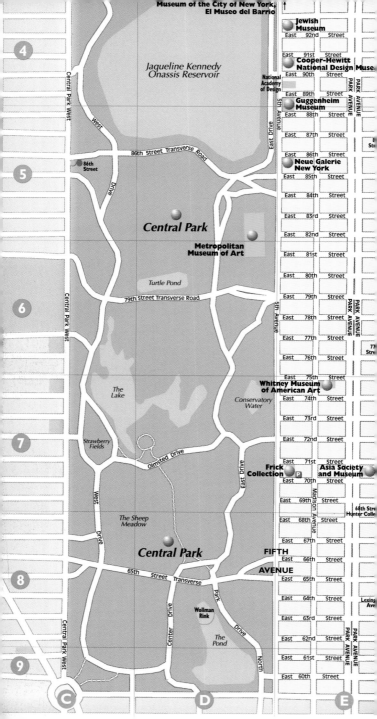

Museum of the City of New York,
El Museo del Barrio

Jewish Museum

East 92nd Street

Cooper-Hewitt
National Design Museum

East 91st Street

East 90th Street

National
Academy
of Design

East 89th Street

Guggenheim
Museum

East 88th Street

East 87th Street

East 86th Street

86th
Street

Neue Galerie
New York

East 85th Street

East 84th Street

Jaqueline Kennedy
Onassis Reservoir

86th Street Transverse Road

East 83rd Street

Central Park

East 82nd Street

Metropolitan
Museum of Art

East 81st Street

East 80th Street

Turtle Pond

East 79th Street

79th Street Transverse Road

East 78th Street

East 77th Street

East 76th Street

East 75th Street

Whitney Museum
of American Art

East 74th Street

The
Lake

Conservatory
Water

East 73rd Street

East 72nd Street

Strawberry
Fields

Olmsted Drive

East 71st Street

Frick
Collection

Asia Society
and Museum

East 70th Street

East 69th Street

64th Street
Hunter College

The Sheep
Meadow

East 68th Street

East 67th Street

Central Park

FIFTH

East 66th Street

AVENUE

65th Street Transverse

East 65th Street

East 64th Street

East 63rd Street

Wollman
Rink

East 62nd Street

The Pond

East 61st Street

East 60th Street

Central Park West

West Drive

5th Avenue

PARK AVENUE

Madison Avenue

Center Drive

Park Drive North

4

5

6

7

8

9

C

D

E

East 93rd Street
UPPER EAST
East 92nd Street
SIDE
East 91st Street

East 90th Street
East 89th Street
East 88th Street
East 87th Street
East 86th Street
East 85th Street
East 84th Street
East 83rd Street
East 82nd Street
East 81st Street
East 80th Street
East 79th Street
East 78th Street
East 77th Street
East 76th Street
East 75th Street
East 74th Street
East 73rd Street
East 72nd Street
East 71st Street
East 70th Street
East 69th Street
East 68th Street
East 67th Street
East 66th Street
East 65th Street
East 64th Street
East 63rd Street
East 62nd Street
East 61st St
East 60th Street

East 91st Street

Gracie Mansion

Carl Schurz Park

John Jay Park

FRANKLIN DELANO ROOSEVELT (FDR) DRIVE

East

3rd Avenue
2nd Avenue
1st Avenue
York Avenue
Lexington Avenue
2ND AVENUE

Mount Vernon Hotel Museum and Garden

HIGHWAY 25   QUEENSBORO BRIDGE

0   300 m
0   250 yds

F   G

Upper East Side & Central Park

Central Park

HIGHLIGHTS

- Delacorte Theater, Shakespeare in the Park
- Summer stage concerts
- Bleachers at Heckscher
- Bethesda Fountain
- Wollman Rink in winter
- Strawberry Fields
- Swedish Cottage Marionette Theater
- Tavern on the Green

TIPS

- Don't walk alone in isolated areas at night.
- Watch out for bicycles on the roads.

The park is the escape valve for the city. Without it New York would overheat—especially in summer, when the humidity tops 90 percent, and bikers, runners, bladers, dog strollers and Frisbee players convene. It's a way of life.

The Greensward Plan In the mid-19th century, when there was no Manhattan north of 42nd Street, *New York Evening Post* editor William Cullen Bryant campaigned until the city invested $5 million in an 840-acre (340ha) wasteland. Responsible for clearing the land was journalist Frederick Law Olmsted, who, with English architect Calvert Vaux, also won the competition to design the park, with his "Greensward Plan." By day, Olmsted supervised the clearance of five million cubic tons of dirt; by night, he and Vaux trod the

Clockwise from top left: take a boat out on the water; joggers and walkers enjoy the surroundings; a view across the lake to some landmark West Side apartments; the memorial to John Lennon in Strawberry Fields; exploring the park on two wheels; picnicking on the grass; strike one

acres and designed. Nighttime walks, though no longer suicidal, are still not advised these days.

Fun and games Start at the Dairy Information Center and pick up a map and events list. These show the layout of the park and tell you about the Wildlife Conservation Center (Zoo), the Carousel, the playgrounds, rinks, fountains, statues and Strawberry Fields, where John Lennon is commemorated close to the Dakota Building where he lived and was shot. But the busy life of the park is not recorded on maps: rollerblade moves on the Mall by the Sheep Meadow; hanging out at the Heckscher Playground and Great Lawn softball leagues; doing the loop road by bike; sunbathing, poolside, at the vast Lasker Pool in Harlem; playing rowboat dodgems on the Lake; or bouldering on the outcrops of Manhattan schist (rock).

THE BASICS

www.centralparknyc.org

✚ D1–D9

☎ 212/794-6564 or 800/201-7275

🕐 Dairy Information Center daily 10–5

🍽 Restaurants, kiosks

🚇 A, B, C, D, 1 59th Street-Columbus Circle; N, Q, R 57th Street-7th Avenue; F 57th Street; 4, 5, 6 86th Street

🚌 M1, M2, M3, M4, M5, M10. Crosstown M66, M30, M72, M86

♿ Moderate

🎫 Free

Cooper-Hewitt National Design Museum

A detail (left) and external view of the Cooper-Hewitt building (right)

THE BASICS

www.cooperhewitt.org
🔲 E4
✉ 2 E 91st Street
☎ 212/849-8400
🕐 Mon–Thu 10–5, Fri 10–9, Sat 10–6, Sun 12–6; closed holidays
🍴 Café
Ⓜ 4, 5, 6 86th Street
🚌 M1, M2, M3, M4
♿ Good
💲 Moderate
❓ Tours available

HIGHLIGHTS

● Paneling in the hall
● Solarium
● Garden
● Architectural drawings
● Summer concerts
● Textiles
● Exhibitions

TIP

● The Shop at Cooper-Hewitt is worth visiting in its own right. Many items from the changing stock are not available elsewhere and the book section is excellent.

The charming Cooper-Hewitt National Design Museum collections are exhibited in an elegant, wood-paneled mansion. When snow falls in the holiday season, there's nowhere better to indulge in mawkishly nostalgic reveries.

Carnegie-Hewitt The mansion belonged to industrialist Andrew Carnegie, who, in 1903, had asked architects Babb, Cook & Willard for "the most modest, plainest and most roomy house in New York City." This he did not receive (aside from the roominess), since this little chateau was built with modern conveniences galore—air-conditioning and elevators—and a big gated garden to keep out the squatter neighbors. The entire neighborhood came to be known as Carnegie Hill. Andrew's wife, Louise, lived here until her death in 1946, then, some 20 years later, the Carnegie Corporation donated it to the Smithsonian Institution to house the Hewitt sisters' collections. The sisters, Amy, Eleanor and Sarah, had become infatuated with London's museums, and this set them collecting.

And Cooper The girls' grandpa Peter Cooper (▷ 38), founder of the Cooper Union college, housed the collection here, where it stayed until 1967. The contemporary Cooper-Hewitt is a vibrant institution where all kinds of events happen. Some of the collections are on display (it's hard to predict which) and there are reference resources, including the US's biggest architectural drawings collection and a textile library.

The Fifth Avenue garden (left) and Fragonard Room (right)

Frick Collection

Like the Wallace Collection in London and the Musée Picasso in Paris, Henry Clay Frick's mansion is half the reason for coming here. Henry bequeathed these riches to the nation as a memorial to himself—that's the kind of guy he was.

The mansion, and the man Henry Clay Frick was chairman of the Carnegie Steel Corp. (US Steel). He was one of the most ruthless strike-breakers of all time and the nastiest industrialist of his day. Instead of any comeuppance (though there were assassination attempts), he got to commission Carrère and Hastings to build him one of the last great Beaux Arts mansions on 5th Avenue and fill it with an exquisite collection of 14th- to 19th-century old masters, porcelain, furniture and bronzes. You can rest in a Louis XVI chair before strolling in the central glass-roofed courtyard and the gorgeous garden.

What Frick bought Some of the 40 rooms are arranged around a particular work or artist, notably the Boucher Room, east of the entrance, and the Fragonard Room, with the *Progress of Love* series. There are British masters (Constable, Gainsborough, Whistler, Turner), Dutch (Vermeer, Rembrandt, Van Eyck, Hals), Italian (Titian, Bellini, Veronese) and Spanish (El Greco, Goya, Velázquez). Interspersed are Limoges enamel and Chinese porcelain, Persian carpets and Marie Antoinette's furniture. Some Frick descendants still have keys to this modest pied à terre, which has a bowling alley in the basement.

THE BASICS

www.frick.org

⊞ E7

✉ 1 E 70th Street

☎ 212/288–0700

🕐 Tue–Sat 10–6, Sun 11–5 10–6; closed holidays

🚇 6 68th Street-Hunter College

🚌 M1, M2, M3, M4

♿ Good

✋ Expensive

❓ Lectures: 1st and 3rd Fri of month 4.30; audio tours

HIGHLIGHTS

● *Mall in St. James's Park*, Gainsborough (1783)

● *Sir Thomas More*, Holbein (1527)

● *Officer and the Laughing Girl*, Vermeer (c1657)

● *The Polish Rider*, Rembrandt (c1655)

● *Virgin and Child with Saints*, Van Eyck (c1441–43)

● *Philip IV of Spain*, Velázquez (1644)

HIGHLIGHTS

● The building
● *L'Hermitage à Pontoise*, Pissarro (1867)
● *Paris Through the Window*, Chagall (1913)
● *Woman Ironing*, Picasso (1904)
● *Nude*, Modigliani (1917)
● Kandinskys
● Klees
● Légers
● The store

TIP

● Consider a City Pass ($79; kids $59). As well as the Gugg, it allows entry to other top attractions. Visit www.citypass.com for information.

If you just happened across Frank Lloyd Wright's space-age rotunda, your eyes would pop out of their sockets, but it's the planet's best-known modern building, so you are prepared. Don't forget the art inside.

Museum of architecture This is the great Frank Lloyd Wright's only New York building. It was commissioned by Solomon R. Guggenheim at the urging of his friend and taste tutor, Baroness Hilla Rebay von Ehrenwiesen, though the wealthy metal-mining magnate died 10 years before it was completed in 1959. The giant white nautilus is certainly arresting, but it's the interior that unleashes the most superlatives. Take the elevator to the top level and snake your way down the museum's spiral ramp to see why. You can study the exhibits,

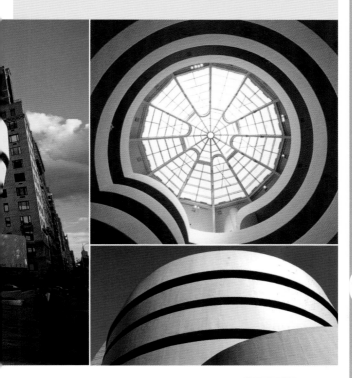

Exterior and interior views of the stunning design by Frank Lloyd Wright

look over the parapet to the lobby below and finish up where you began.

Museum of art There are around 6,000 pieces in the Guggenheim Foundation's possession. Solomon R. and his wife Irene Rothschild abandoned the old masters they sought at first, when Hilla Rebay introduced them to Léger, Kandinsky, Mondrian and Moholy-Nagy, Chagall and Gleizes, and they got hooked on the moderns. See also the early Picassos in the small rotunda and the 1992 tower extension. If you like the Impressionists and Postimpressionists, look for the Thannhauser Collection, always on display—unlike the rotated Guggenheim holdings. The Guggenheim continues to acquire works of art, including Agathe Snow's *Goldfinch* (2008), fashioned from debris found on local streets.

THE BASICS

www.guggenheim.org
✚ E4
✉ 1071 5th Avenue/
89th Street
☎ 212/423-3500
🕐 Sun–Wed, Fri 10–5.45,
Sat 10–7.45; closed Dec 25
🍴 Café
🚇 4, 5, 6 86th Street
🚌 M1, M2, M3, M4
♿ Good
💲 Expensive
❓ Lecture program;
audio tours

Metropolitan Museum of Art

HIGHLIGHTS

● Temple of Dendur (15BC)
● Period rooms, American Wing
● 19th- and early 20th-century art galleries
● *Young Woman with a Water Jug*, Vermeer (c1662)
● *Reading at a Table*, Picasso (1934)

TIP

● Consider visiting on Friday or Saturday evening, when a string quartet serenades you and there are far fewer crowds.

It will give you bigger blisters than the Uffizi, bigger chills than the Sistine Chapel and take a bigger slice of vacation time than all dinners. It's so big that it doesn't just contain Egyptian artifacts but an entire Egyptian building.

Art city The limestone Beaux Arts facade with its tremendous steps was a 1902 addition to the Calvert Vaux (of Central Park fame) redbrick Gothic building buried inside. There are several more buildings-within-buildings, interior gardens and courtyards, such is the scale of the Met. The 15BC Temple of Dendur, in its glass-walled bemoated chamber east of the main entrance, is the best known, but there's much more besides: the Astor Court above it—a replica Ming dynasty scholar's courtyard—plus, in the American Wing, a

The outside steps on a busy summer day (left); inside the main entrance of the museum with the information desk at the center (right)

score of period-style rooms, and the vast and sunlighted garden court with its hodgepodge of Tiffany glass and topiary, a Frank Lloyd Wright window and the entire Federal-style facade of the United States Bank from Wall Street.

Where to start? How to stop? A quarter of the 3 million-plus objects are up at any one time, so pace yourself. Relax. There are about 23 distinct collections. Some visitors decide on one or two per visit—Egyptian art, for example, or the new galleries for 19th- and early-20th-century European paintings which contain one of the largest Impressionist collections outside Paris. Or you could structure a route around one or two favorite works. On the ground level, the Information Center in the Uris Center, with its Orientation Theater and giant floor plans, is the place to begin.

THE BASICS

www.metmuseum.org

✚ D5

✉ 1000 5th Avenue/82nd Street

☎ 212/535-7710

🕐 Tue–Thu, Sun 9.30–5.30, Fri, Sat 9.30–9

🍴 Cafeteria, restaurant, bar

🚇 4, 5, 6 86th Street

🚌 M1, M2, M3, M4

♿ Good

👋 Expensive

❓ The Cloisters (▷ 106) houses more of the Met's medieval collections; same-day admission on Met ticket

Whitney Museum of American Art

HIGHLIGHTS

● Biennial
● *Circus*, Alexander Calder (1926–31)
● The Hoppers
● The O'Keeffes
● *Dempsey and Firpo*, George Bellows (1924)
● The Louise Nevelsons
● Drawbridge

TIP

● Come Friday from 6pm to 9pm. Admission is pay-what-you-wish and there are live musical performances.

More modern than the Modern, the Whitney wants to be as unpredictable as the *artist du jour* and very often succeeds. It's a New York tradition to sneer at the Biennial, whether or not you have seen the show.

No room at the Met Sculptor and patron of her contemporaries' work, Gertrude Vanderbilt Whitney offered her collection to the Met in 1929, but the great institution turned up its nose and Whitney was forced to found the Whitney. In 1966, Marcel Breuer's cantilevered, granite-clad Brutalist block was completed to house it in a suitably controversial manner—a building that is not universally loved but impossible to overlook. The Whitney's core collection now reads like a roll call of American 20th-century greats: Edward Hopper, Thomas Hart

Visitors at the information and entry desks of the Whitney Museum of American Art

Benton, Willem de Kooning, Georgia O'Keeffe, Claes Oldenburg, Jasper Johns, George Bellows and Jackson Pollock are a few. Let's hope the curators and buyers are as good as Gertrude at spotting talent.

Take your pick Exhibitions, drawn from the museum's important and delicious collection, often emphasize a single artist's work. At other times they prove more eclectic. There's an active film and video department, and although the branch at the Altria Building closed in 2008, there are plans for a new building in the Meatpacking District. The Whitney Biennial (in the spring of even-numbered years) offers an echo of those days, when the New York art pack gets sweaty debating the merits and demerits of the chosen few on show and of the curator's vision.

THE BASICS

www.whitney.org

➕ E7

✉ 945 Madison Avenue/ 75th Street

☎ 212/570-3600

🕐 Wed–Thu, Sat–Sun 11–6, Fri 1–9; closed Thanksgiving, Dec 25, Jan 1

🍴 Café

🚇 6 77th Street

🚌 M1, M2, M3, M4

♿ Good

💵 Expensive

❓ Exhibitions, events; free daily tours

More to See

ASIA SOCIETY AND MUSEUM
www.asiasociety.org
This collection of Asian art and culture is based on that started by John D. Rockefeller III.
✚ E7 ✉ 725 Park Avenue/70th Street
☎ 212/288-6400 🕐 Tue–Sun 11–6, Fri 11–9 🚇 6 68th Street 🖐 Moderate

GRACIE MANSION
Gracie Mansion has been the mayor's official residence since 1942 though Mayor Bloomberg declined it. Built in 1799, it was then a remote country house. Reservations required for tours.
✚ G4–G5 ✉ East End Avenue/88th Street
☎ 212/639-9675 🚇 4, 5, 6 86th Street
🖐 Moderate

JEWISH MUSEUM
www.thejewishmuseum.org
The largest Jewish museum in the Western hemisphere chronicling Jewish experience worldwide.
✚ E4 ✉ 1109 5th Avenue/92nd Street
☎ 212/423-3200 🕐 Daily 11–5.45 (closed Wed; seasons vary, check) 🍴 Café 🚇 4, 5, 6 86th Street 🖐 Expensive; free Sat

EL MUSEO DEL BARRIO
www.elmuseo.org
New York's only museum dedicated to Latin American and Caribbean art and culture with over 8,000 items.
✚ E2 ✉ 1230 5th Avenue/104th Street
☎ 212/831-7272 🕐 Wed–Sun 11–6
🚇 6 103rd Street 🖐 Donation (moderate)

MUSEUM OF THE CITY OF NEW YORK
www.mcny.org
Rotating exhibitions illustrating the changing life of the city dating back to 1624. Special walking tours available.
✚ E2 ✉ 1220 5th Avenue/103rd Street
☎ 212/534-1672 🕐 Tue–Sun 10–5 🚇 6 103rd Street 🖐 Donation (moderate)

NEUE GALERIE NEW YORK
www.neuegalerie.org
Dedicated to early-20th-century German and Austrian art and design, this gallery has marvelous collections of paintings and other media.
✚ E5 ✉ 1048 5th Avenue/86th Street
☎ 212/628-6200 🕐 Thu–Mon 11–6
🚇 4, 5, 6 86th Street 🖐 Expensive

Museum of the City of New York

Gracie Mansion bathed in winter sunshine

Shopping

BARNEYS

Many are the New Yorkers who dress exclusively from the *ne plus ultra* of high-fashion stores. Over several floors find avant-garde designers, own label clothes, the city's best high-end cosmetics and scent departments, every hip jeans label, menswear, epic shoe departments, directional jewelry, homewares, kids' clothes and more. Prices are high.
➕ E9 ✉ 660 Madison Avenue/61st Street ☎ 212/826-8900 🚇 N, R 5th Avenue/59th Street

BLOOMINGDALE'S

Bloomingdale's, opened in 1879, is one of the most venerable names in Manhattan yet keeps up with every trend. The jewelry and handbag sections are excellent.
➕ F9 ✉ 1000 3rd Avenue/59th Street ☎ 212/705-2000 🚇 4, 5, 6, F, N, R 59th Street

CALVIN KLEIN

The iconic New York designer's flagship store, designed by David Chipperfield, is as spare and minimal as his clothing without even racks to spoil the clean lines (you point at a display and request your size). His home line is downstairs.
➕ E9 ✉ 654 Madison Avenue/60th Street ☎ 212/292-9000 🚇 N, R 5th Avenue/59th Street

DI MODOLO

The Milanese jewellery company has arrived in Manhattan—and with Catherine Zeta Jones as its new "face." Expect luxury watches (with prices to match) inlaid with precious stones, vibrant coloured gemstone creations, and for the guys, a collection that includes understated but eye-catching cuff links and bracelets.
➕ E8 ✉ 703 Madison Avenue, between 62nd and 63rd ☎ 212/644-6564 🚇 F to Lexington Avenue/63rd Street

DONNA KARAN

This beautiful bilevel space carries the home line, accessories and the best of new season Karan, as well as her lower-price lines.
➕ E8 ✉ 819 Madison Avenue/E 68th Street

☎ 212/861-1001 🚇 6 68th Street-Hunter College

KITCHEN ARTS AND LETTERS

This is a treasure trove of cookbooks by leading authors including James Beard and Julia Child.
➕ E4 ✉ 1435 Lexington Avenue, between 93rd and 94th streets ☎ 212/876-5550 🚇 6 96th Street

RALPH LAUREN

Distinguished cowboy and English country heritage looks in the Rhinelander Mansion, one of a few of such turn-of-the-20th-century houses in Manhattan.
➕ E7 ✉ 867 Madison Avenue, between E 71st and 72nd streets ☎ 212/606-2100 🚇 6 68th Street-Hunter College

SHANGHAI TANG

Youthful Asian-style clothing.
➕ E8 ✉ 600 Madison Avenue ☎ 212/888-0111 🚇 F Lexington Avenue-63rd Street

ZITOMER

At root, an über-drugstore, this Upper East Side classic has grown to encompass everything from toys to pet accessories. The number of bath, body and skincare ranges is impressive and it's the best place to shop for hair ornaments.
➕ E6 ✉ 969 Madison Avenue/76th Street ☎ 212/737-5560 🚇 6 77th Street

Entertainment and Nightlife

92ND STREET Y

www.927.org

A varied program of events includes readings by renowned authors, folk, jazz and lectures that cover a wide range of subjects. Celebrated its 125th anniversary in 1999.

⊞ E4 ☒ Kauffman Concert Hall, 1395 Lexington Avenue/92nd Street ☎ 212/415-5500 🚇 6 96th Street

CAFÉ CARLYLE

www.thecarlyle.com

This lounge in the elegant Carlyle Hotel was home to the great Bobby Short, until his death in 2005, but his spirit lives on in the piano player lounge singers and jazz bands. Be sure to look in at Bemelman's Bar.

⊞ E6 ☒ Carlyle Hotel, Madison Avenue/76th Street ☎ 212/744-1600 🚇 6 77th Street

CAFÉ PIERRE

Jazz and cabaret songs, plus requests, from Nancy Winston and Kathleen Landis.

⊞ E9 ☒ 5th Avenue/61st Street ☎ 212/838-8000 🚇 N, R 5th Avenue/59th Street

DANGERFIELD'S

www.dangerfields.com

This club, established in 1969, is going strong. Those who have performed here include Jay Leno and Jim Carrey.

⊞ F9 ☒ 1118 1st Avenue/61st Street ☎ 212/593-1650 🚇 4, 5, 6 59th Street

FEINSTEINS AT THE REGENCY

www.feinsteinsattheregency.com

The cabaret star Michael Feinstein himself performs at his namesake venue only a couple of times a year but the rest of the time he manages to secure top Broadway names for this swanky, intimate room.

⊞ E9 ☒ Regency Hotel, 540 Park Avenue/61st Street ☎ 212/339-4095 🚇 N, R Lexington Avenue/59th Street

FLORENCE GOULD HALL

The 400-seat venue is associated with the Alliance Française. The range of events takes in opera, pop singers, dance, jazz and readings.

⊞ E9 ☒ 55 E 59th Street/Park–Madison avenues ☎ 212/355-6100 🚇 N, R 5th Avenue/59th Street

OUT IN CENTRAL PARK

Central Park is a welcoming park. For those who crave physical activity there's lots to do.

Bike Riding You can rent a no-frills bicycle.

Roller Blading Skate rental and lessons are available at Wollman Rink.

Ice Skating Wollman Rink rents figure skates and hockey skates and is an ice rink in winter.

Running The park is the most popular place for running and jogging.

GRACE RAINEY ROGERS AUDITORIUM

www.metmuseum.org

A 700-seat auditorium for musical groups. Chamber music is played in the great hall balcony of the Met on Friday and Saturday evenings.

⊞ D5 ☒ Metropolitan Museum of Art, 1000 5th Avenue/82nd Street ☎ 212/570-3949 🚇 4, 5, 6 86th Street

ROOF GARDEN CAFÉ AND MARTINI BAR AT THE MET

You can get cocktails and simple food on this rooftop terrace with bits of its sponsors' sculpture collection among the wisteria trellises and a heavenly view of Central Park treetops. It's one of the nicest places for an early drink in New York. Access is by elevators on the far southwest corner. Open May through late fall (weather permitting).

⊞ D5 ☒ Metropolitan Museum of Art, 1000 5th Avenue/82nd Street ☎ 212/535-7710 🚇 6 86th Street

STONE ROSES LOUNGE

Good company, impressive design elements, fine food and drink and, most importantly, stunning, sweeping views of Central Park and Broadway.

⊞ C9 ☒ 10 Times Warner Center, Columbus Circle ☎ 212 823 9769 🚇 A, B, C, D 59th Street/Columbus Circle

Restaurants

PRICES

Prices are approximate, based on a 3-course meal for one person.

$$$	over $60
$$	$40–$60
$	under $40

BOAT HOUSE ($$)

www.thecentralparkboathouse.com

Leave Manhattan entirely at this unique lakeside place in Central Park. The food is contemporary American but the view is the point. The cocktail deck gets busy in summer. Booking advised.

➕ D7 ⊠ Central Park, nearest to E 72nd Street entrance ☎ 212/517-2233 🕐 Closed major holidays and dinner Dec–Mar 🚇 6 68th Street-Hunter College

CAFÉ BOULUD ($$–$$$)

www.cafeboulud.com

A favorite Daniel Boulud restaurant where three muses inspire the menu—classics, seasons and ethnic cuisines. You will find *pot au feu*, *bouilla-baisse* and entrées inspired by Tuscany, Spain, Morocco and Vietnam.

➕ E6 ⊠ 20 E 76th Street/5th–Madison avenues ☎ 212/772-2600 🕐 Closed Mon lunch and major holidays 🚇 6 77th Street

CAFÉ SABARSKY ($–$$)

www.wallse.com

Much more than a museum café, this—fittingly for somewhere in the patrician town house that is the Neue Galerie—looks like a 1920s Viennese Kaffeehaus and has New York's premier Austrian chef, Kurt Gutenbrunner at the helm. You can also just drop in for the *Kaffee und Kuchen*.

➕ E5 ⊠ Neue Galerie New York, 1048 5th Avenue/86th Street ☎ 212/288-0665 🕐 Closed Tue and major holidays 🚇 4, 5, 6 86th Street

DANIEL ($$$)

www.danielnyc.com

Perhaps the most formal restaurant in the city, with its salmon-pink walls and columned arches. Serves exquisitely restrained, modern French dishes—opt for the degustation menu to fully appreciate chef Daniel Boulud's brilliance. Dessert arrives

TAVERN ON THE GREEN

The Tavern delivers a memorable dining experience despite its stature as a tourist destination (colored glass, lanterns, topiary…), and despite the breadth of its menu, which ranges from prime rib with Yorkshire pudding to sautéed rainbow trout. In summer you can dance under the stars in the garden from 9pm.

➕ C8 ⊠ Central Park West/67th Street ☎ 212/873-3200 🚇 1 66th Street-Lincoln Center

with its own "basket" of warm madeleines.

➕ E8 ⊠ 60 E 65th Street/Madison–Park avenues ☎ 212/288-0033 🕐 Closed Sun 🚇 6 68th Street-Hunter College

JACKSON HOLE ($)

www.jacksonholeburgers.com

This small chain of burger places is useful when all you want is a hefty sandwich in a child-friendly, no-frills environment.

➕ E4 ⊠ 1270 Madison Avenue/91st Street ☎ 212/427-2820 🚇 4, 5, 6 86th Street

➕ F8 ⊠ 232 E 64th Street/2nd Avenue ☎ 212/371-7187 🕐 Closed major holidays 🚇 6 68th Street-Hunter College

OAK ROOM ($$–$$$)

www.oakroomny.com

Relaunched with rising star Eric Hara at the helm, the blend is an eclectic choice of menus and New York of a bygone glamour.

➕ D9 ⊠ Plaza Hotel, 10 Central Park South ☎ 212/758-7777 🚇 N, R to 5th Avenue/59th Street

SERENDIPITY 3 ($)

www.serendipity3.com

This toy box/candy store makes the original and best "Frozen Hot Chocolate." You don't need a child in tow but you do need a sweet tooth.

➕ F9 ⊠ 225 E 60th Street/2nd Avenue ☎ 212/838-3531 🚇 4, 5, 6 59th Street

West of Central Park is a largely residential, pleasantly leafy neighborhood of grand apartment buildings and big brownstones. Its major attraction is Lincoln Center, with world-class performances.

Sights	**92–95**
Walk	**96**
Shopping	**97**
Entertainment and Nightlife	**99**
Restaurants	**100**

Top 25	**TOP 25**
American Museum of Natural History ▷ **92**	
Lincoln Center ▷ **94**	

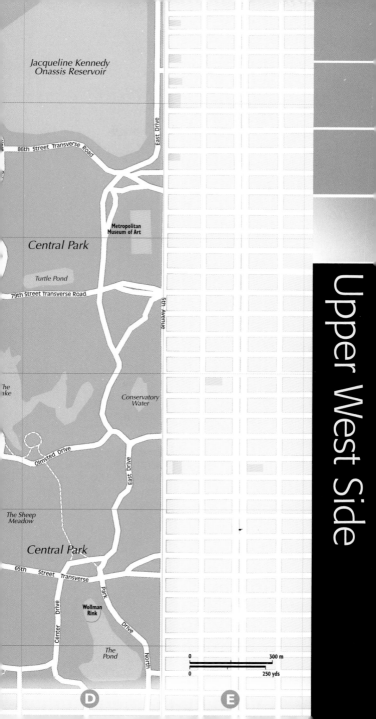

Jacqueline Kennedy
Onassis Reservoir

86th Street Transverse Road

East Drive

Metropolitan
Museum of Art

Central Park

Turtle Pond

79th Street Transverse Road

5th Avenue

The
Lake

Conservatory
Water

Olmsted Drive

East Drive

The Sheep
Meadow

Central Park

65th Street Transverse

Center Drive

Park Drive

Wollman
Rink

The
Pond

North

Upper West Side

0   300 m
0   250 yds

D   E

American Museum of Natural History

HIGHLIGHTS

- Blue whale
- Barosaurus
- Cape York Meteorite
- Dinosaur halls
- Journey to the Stars
- Star of India
- The dioramas
- Dinosaur embryo
- Monthly drinks and dancing at the Rose Center

TIP

● You can observe the entire life cycle of tropical butterflies from October to June at the Butterfly Conservatory.

No longer a lovable anachronism since its renovation, this 19th-century hulk is stuffed with dinosaur skeletons and appended by the amazing Rose Center. The blue whale's cocktail bar and the dioramas are delightful.

Who's who Of the 36 million items owned by the museum—the largest such institution in the world—only a small fraction is on show. Among the improvements funded by a $45-million cash injection were a sprucing-up of the buildings themselves and, most notably, the metamorphosed Hayden Planetarium, in the Rose Center, next door, with its thrill ride through the universe. There's far too much to see in one day, with three city blocks and the entire evolution of life on earth covered. Not-to-be-missed items include the

The dinosaurs are always popular, especially with children (left); the entrance of the museum (right)

barosaurus rearing up to her full 55ft (17m) to protect her young from a T-Rex attack and the 94ft (29m) blue whale that dominates the two-story Hall of Ocean Life and Biology of Fishes.

More gems Another highlight is the 563-carat Star of India sapphire, part of the unbelievable Hall of Meteorites, Minerals and Gems, containing almost $50-million worth of precious stones, plus Cape York meteorite. The cutest part of the museum is where animals of all sizes are displayed behind glass in *tableaux morts* of great artistic merit. In the Lefrak Imax Theater a 44ft (14m) screen shows ecological blockbusters, but it's the new planetarium, where visitors are transported to the beginning of time and space with the recreation of the "Big Bang," that takes the cake.

THE BASICS

www.amnh.org

➕ C6

✉ Central Park West/ 79th Street

☎ 212/769-5100

🕐 Daily 10–5.45; closed holidays

🍽 Various

Ⓜ B, C 81st Street- Museum of Natural History

🚌 M7, M10, M11, M79, M86, M104

♿ Good

💲 Expensive

❓ 1-hour tours from 10.15 until 3.15. Rose Center drinks and dancing 2nd Friday of month, 9pm–1am ☎ 212/769- 5200 for advance reservations for special exhibits, films, etc.

Lincoln Center

HIGHLIGHTS

● Chandeliers in the Met foyer and auditorium
● Reflecting Pool with Henry Moore's *Reclining Figure* (1965)
● Lincoln Center Out-of-Doors Festival
● NY City Ballet's *Nutcracker*
● Chagall murals, Met foyer
● NY Philharmonic's free dress rehearsals, Avery Fisher Hall
● New York Film Festival
● Redsigned Philip Johnson's Plaza fountain
● Jazz at Lincoln Center
● Annual Messiah singalong

TIP

● Dance under the stars at the Midsummer Night's Swing in Josie Robertson Plaza, a free summertime series of live band sessions.

Strolling to the fantastically fairy-lighted 10-story Metropolitan Opera House colonnade across the Central Plaza on a winter's night is one of the most glamorous things you can do in this city, and you don't need tickets.

West Side Story The Rockefeller-funded über-arts center was envisaged in the late 1950s and finished in 1969, after 7,000 families and 800 businesses had been pushed aside by developer Robert Moses and the John D. Rockefeller millions. Much of *West Side Story* was filmed here after the demolition began.

All the arts The 15 acres (6ha) include mega-houses for the biggest-scale arts, all designed by different architects in the same white travertine. The

Lincoln Center at night, with one of the Marc Chagall murals visible behind the left-hand arch (left); Christmas decorations add sparkle to the Central Plaza (right)

Metropolitan Opera House is the glamour queen, with her vast Marc Chagall murals, red carpet, swooshes of stair and chandeliers that thrillingly rise to the gold-leaf ceiling before performances. You can take a fascinating back stage tour. Avery Fisher Hall is home to America's oldest orchestra, the NY Philharmonic, while the Juilliard School of Music supplies it with fresh talent. The David H. Koch Theater, housing the New York City Opera and the New York City Ballet, faces Avery Fisher across the Plaza. The Franklin P. Rose Hall is the centerpiece of jazz at Lincoln Center in the Time Warner Center. Two smaller theaters, the Vivian Beaumont and Mitzi New-house, and a more intimate concert hall, Alice Tully, plus the Walter Reade movie theater and the little Bruno Walter Auditorium, complete the pack. Renovation took place in 2009, in time to celebrate its 50th anniversary.

THE BASICS

www.lincolncenter.org
⊞ B8
⊠ 70 Lincoln Center Plaza
☎ 212/875-5000
Met 212/362-6000
Avery Fisher Hall
212/875-5030
Jazz 212/258-9800
🕐 Inquire for performance times
🍽 Restaurants, cafés, bars
🚇 1 66th Street-Lincoln Center
🚌 M5, M7, M10, M11, M104, crosstown M66
♿ Good
🎟 Admission to Center free
❓ Tours leave from David Rubenstein Atrium, daily 10–4 ☎ 212/875-5456

A Walk on the West Side

From grand apartment buildings, stylish boutiques and fine dining to the cultural treasure chest that is the Lincoln Center.

DISTANCE: 1.5 miles (2.5km)   **ALLOW:** 40 minutes

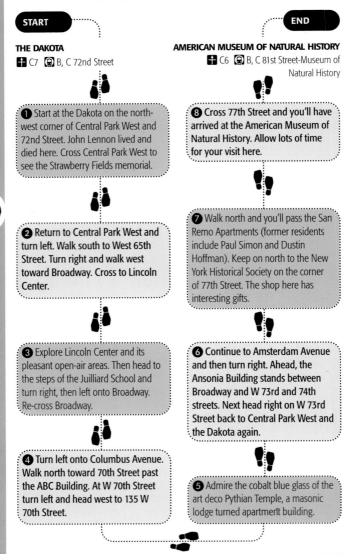

START

THE DAKOTA
⊞ C7 ⊙ B, C 72nd Street

END

AMERICAN MUSEUM OF NATURAL HISTORY
⊞ C6 ⊙ B, C 81st Street-Museum of Natural History

1 Start at the Dakota on the north-west corner of Central Park West and 72nd Street. John Lennon lived and died here. Cross Central Park West to see the Strawberry Fields memorial.

8 Cross 77th Street and you'll have arrived at the American Museum of Natural History. Allow lots of time for your visit here.

2 Return to Central Park West and turn left. Walk south to West 65th Street. Turn right and walk west toward Broadway. Cross to Lincoln Center.

7 Walk north and you'll pass the San Remo Apartments (former residents include Paul Simon and Dustin Hoffman). Keep on north to the New York Historical Society on the corner of 77th Street. The shop here has interesting gifts.

3 Explore Lincoln Center and its pleasant open-air areas. Then head to the steps of the Juilliard School and turn right, then left onto Broadway. Re-cross Broadway.

6 Continue to Amsterdam Avenue and then turn right. Ahead, the Ansonia Building stands between Broadway and W 73rd and 74th streets. Next head right on W 73rd Street back to Central Park West and the Dakota again.

4 Turn left onto Columbus Avenue. Walk north toward 70th Street past the ABC Building. At W 70th Street turn left and head west to 135 W 70th Street.

5 Admire the cobalt blue glass of the art deco Pythian Temple, a masonic lodge turned apartment building.

WALK

UPPER WEST SIDE

Shopping

BARNES AND NOBLE

This is one of the megabook chain's main New York branches. There's usually an evening reading.

+ B5 ✉ 2289 Broadway/82nd Street ☎ 212/362-8835, and branches ⒬ 1 79th Street

BETSEY JOHNSON

This long-lived fashion darling produces fun looks.

+ C7 ✉ 248 Columbus Avenue/71st Street ☎ 212/362-3364 ⒬ 1, 2, 3, B, C 72nd Street

BLUEMERCURY APOTHECARY & SPA

From the top brand cosmetics to spa services hair care and famous fragrances, Bluemercury is a welcome addition to the Upper West Side retail offering.

+ B5 ✉ 2305 Broadway (83rd Street) ☎ 212/799-0500 ⒬ 1 to 86th Street

FAIRWAY

Get a taste of Upper West Side everyday life at this bewilderingly comprehensive grocery.

+ B7 ✉ 2127 Broadway/75th Street ☎ 212/595-1888 ⒬ 1, 2, 3 72nd Street

KENNETH COLE

Quality shoes ranging from urban footwear to trendy fashion styles, and simple but stylish clothes for women and men, plus handbags, jewelry, sunglasses and many

other accessories.

+ B6 ✉ 353 Columbus Avenue between W 76th and 77th streets ☎ 212/873-2061 ⒬ 1 79th Street

LAILA ROWE

This is one of a growing chain-ette of accessories stores, crammed with colorful gear. Expect a fun vibe and fast-changing selections of jewelry at prices that belie their on-the-money directional style.

+ C7 ✉ 253 Columbus Avenue/72nd Street ☎ 212/579-5254 ⒬ B, C, 1, 2, 3 72nd Street

MALIA MILLS

The boutique swimwear emporium cherished by every woman who's ever loathed her reflection: there are mix-and-match pieces made to fit everyone—and they're super-cool, too.

+ C7 ✉ 220 Columbus

SUMMER IN THE CITY

One of the best reasons to brave the summer heat is for the wonderful selection of free entertainment put on by many of the city's premier cultural institutions. Without paying a dime it's possible to enjoy alfresco operas, theater, art, eating, jazz, classical music, movies, dance, rock-and-roll, blues and folk music. Many arrive early for big performances and stake out a spot for a picnic.

Avenue/70th Street ☎ 212/874-7200 ⒬ 1, 2, 3, B, C 72nd Street

PATAGONIA

If you like social and environmental consciousness with your outdoor wear but still want to look slick while climbing the mountain, swimming the Channel or just look like you might have done so, then this is your place.

+ C6 ✉ 426 Columbus Avenue/81st Street ☎ 917/441-0011 ⒬ B, C 81st Street-Museum of Natural History

STEVEN ALAN

The Lower East Side look on the Upper West Side: This is a carefully edited array of the most cutting-edge small hipsters' labels, some of them available nowhere else—including Alan's own designs.

+ B5 ✉ 465 Amsterdam Avenue/82nd Street ☎ 212/595-8451 ⒬ 1, 2, 3, 79th Street/Broadway; A, C, E 81st Street/Central Park West

ZABAR'S

This is the pleasantly wise-cracking New Yawker of the foodie havens with a Jewish soul all its own. Cheese, coffee, smoked fish and the like are downstairs, while upstairs are the city's best buys in kitchenwares.

+ B6 ✉ 2245 Broadway/80th Street ☎ 212/787-2000 ⒬ 1 79th Street

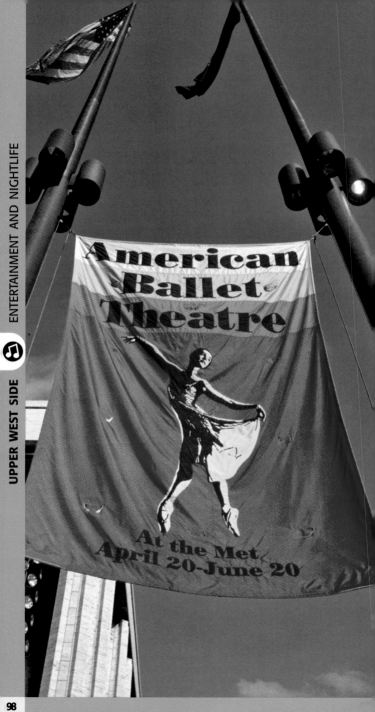

Entertainment and Nightlife

AVERY FISHER HALL

www.new.lincolncenter.org
The home of the New York Philharmonic seats 2,700. The hall is also home to other groups including the American Symphony Orchestra.
🚇 B8 ✉ 10 Lincoln Center Plaza, Columbus Avenue/65th Street ☎ 212/875-5030 🚇 1 66th Street-Lincoln Center

BEACON THEATRE

www.beacontheatre.com
Storytelling, readings, children's performance, music, dance and more.
🚇 B7 ✉ 2124 Broadway/74th Street ☎ 212/465-6500 🚇 1, 2, 3 72nd Street

BRUNO WALTER AUDITORIUM

Seminars, lectures, films and concerts.
🚇 B8 ✉ The New York Library for the Performing Arts, 111 Amsterdam Avenue between 64th and 65th streets ☎ 212/642-0142 🚇 1 66th Street-Lincoln Center

CATHEDRAL CHURCH OF ST. JOHN THE DIVINE

The Cathedral provides a program of liturgical, cultural and civic events.
🚇 B1 ✉ 1047 Amsterdam Avenue/112th Street ☎ 212/316-7540 🚇 1 Cathedral Parkway/110th Street

DIZZY'S CLUB COCA COLA

www.jalc.org/dccc
Jazz at Lincoln Center's intimate club is—in the spirit of Dizzy Gillespie—

designed to ensure that performers and spectators alike *relaaaaax*. There are also After Hours sets Tuesday through Saturday nights.
🚇 C9 ✉ Time Warner Center at Broadway/60th Street, 5th floor ☎ 212/258-9595 🚇 A, B, C, D, 1 59th Street-Columbus Circle

LINCOLN PLAZA CINEMAS

www.lincolnplazacinema.com
Six screens showing successful first runs and foreign movies.
🚇 B8 ✉ 1886 Broadway/63rd Street ☎ 212/757-2280 🚇 1 66th Street-Lincoln Center

THE METROPOLITAN OPERA

www.metoperafamily.org
The gala openings at this world-class opera rank among the most glamorous of the city's cultural events. Serious buffs line up on Saturday mornings

for inexpensive standing-room tickets. The season runs October to April.
🚇 B8 ✉ 30 Lincoln Center ☎ 212/362-6000 🚇 1 66th Street-Lincoln Center

NEW YORK CITY OPERA

www.nyopera.com
The repertoire of this fine opera company, the Met's neighbor, incorporates a wider variety including newer works, operetta and musicals.
🚇 B8 ✉ David H. Koch Theater, 20 Lincoln Center ☎ 212/870-5570 🚇 1 66th Street-Lincoln Center

SMOKE

www.smokejazz.com
Plush couches adorn this intimate lounge, which hosts great jazz artists and local favorites.
🚇 B2 ✉ 2751 Broadway/105th Street ☎ 212/864-6662 🚇 1 103rd Street

STAND UP NEW YORK

www.standupny.com
Traditional comedy club where new and aspiring comics test their routines.
🚇 B6 ✉ 236 W 78th Street/Broadway ☎ 212/595-0850 🚇 1 79th Street

SYMPHONY SPACE

www.symphonyspace.org
Storytelling, readings, children's theater, music, film, dance and more.
🚇 B4 ✉ 2537 Broadway/95th Street ☎ 212/864-5400 🚇 1, 2, 3 96th Street

Restaurants

AIX ($$$)

www.aixnyc.com
Didier Virot has brought his own style of robust Provençal cuisine to the Upper West Side at this busy tri-level restaurant. Typical dishes are Thyme-citrus smoked brisket and crispy *dorade* (sea bream) with Parmesan crust.
➕ B5 ✉ 2398 Broadway/ 88th Street ☎ 212/874-7400 🕐 Closed lunch; open for Sun brunch 🚇 1 86th Street

BARNEY GREENGRASS ($)

www.barneygreengrass.com
An Upper West Side tradition since 1929, this is frantic on weekends, when locals feast on huge platters of smoked fish—whitefish, sable, sturgeon and lox—or sandwiches made with similar contents.
➕ B5 ✉ 541 Amsterdam Avenue/86th Street ☎ 212/724-4707 🕐 Closed Mon 🚇 1 86th Street

BOAT BASIN CAFÉ ($)

www.boatbasincafe.com
It's hard to find this totally unpretentious place practically on the banks of the Hudson, but if you do, it's worth waiting for a terrace table. The food is dinerlike, but you'll be dazzled by the view.
➕ A6 ✉ W 79th Street/ Hudson River ☎ 212/496-5542 🚇 1 79th Street

CARMINE'S ($$)

www.carminesnyc.com
Join the mob scene here—no, it's not actually anything to do with the Mafia, but this beloved, raucous place does serve its Sicilian-Italian dishes family-style—huge platters to share. It's not for picky foodies, but it's fun.
➕ B4 ✉ 2450 Broadway/ 90th Street ☎ 212/362-2200 🚇 1, 2, 3 96th Street/Broadway

FATTY CRAB ($$)

www.fattycrab.com
Malaysia meets Manhattan in this unpre-tentious newish arrival. The menu is imaginative, and it's not exclusively seafood—the short rib rending is extremely good. Another branch in the West Village.
➕ B6 ✉ 2170 Broadway,

between 76th and 77th ☎ 212/496-2722 🚇 1 to Broadway/79th Street

JEAN-GEORGES ($$$)

www.jean-georges.com
One of the world's great chefs, Alsace native Jean Georges Vongerichten's refined, full-flavored Asian-accented style cannot be imitated. The glass-walled minimalist rooms feel serene and special—perhaps because they were Feng-Shui-ed? Don't miss the molten-center chocolate cake.
➕ C9 ✉ 1 Central Park West ☎ 212/299-3900 🕐 Closed Sat lunch, Sun 🚇 A, C, 1, B, D 59th Street-Columbus Circle

OUEST ($$–$$$)

www.ouest.com
This place single-handedly revitalized the moribund Upper West Side dining scene—with its red booths and the inspired Euro-American posh comfort dishes of chef Tom Valenti. His lamb shanks are legendary.
➕ B5 ✉ 2315 Broadway/ 83rd Street ☎ 212/580-8700 🚇 1 86th Street

PICHOLINE ($$$)

www.picholinenyc.com
The Mediterranean cuisine of Terrance Brennan is as good as it ever was at his first New York address.
➕ C8 ✉ 35 W 64th Street, between Central Park West and Broadway ☎ 212/724-8585 🕐 Closed lunch, Sun 🚇 1 66th Street-Lincoln Center

New York extends far beyond Manhattan and its outer boroughs are increasingly attractive to those who seek a more relaxed approach to life. Brooklyn especially has plenty to engage visitors.

Sights	104–107	Top 25	**TOP 25**
Restaurants	108	Brooklyn ▷ 104	

Brooklyn

HIGHLIGHTS

● Smith Street restaurants
● Brooklyn Heights Promenade
● Bandshell concerts
● The Theater and Rose Cinema at BAM
● Houses in the Heights
● The Art Museum

TIP

● Best of Brooklyn Food Tasting and Multicultural Neighborhood tours operate three times a week (pick-up Greenwich Village; www.newyorkfuntours.com).

Brooklyn has it all—one of the largest art museums in the US and some of New York's best restaurants; beaches and a park; a zoo, aquarium and children's museum; hip neighborhoods and avant-garde arts.

Big, bigger, biggest If Brooklyn were still a separate city, it would be the fourth largest in the US. Home to more than 2 million people, it is the most populous of New York's boroughs and the most diverse, with Russian, Middle Eastern, Italian, West Indian, Hasidic Jewish and Chinese neighborhoods. The Brooklyn Museum of Art, intended by McKim, Mead & White to be the biggest museum in the world (it's actually the seventh largest in the US), has collections ranging from pre-Columbian art to 58 Rodin sculptures, plus what many feel

Remsen Street in Brooklyn Heights (left); Brooklyn Bridge seen from Seaport Pier, Manhattan (right)

THE BASICS

Brooklyn Heights
➕ H22
🚇 2, 3 Clark Street

Brooklyn Museum of Art
www.brooklynmuseum.org
➕ Off map to southeast
✉ 200 Eastern Parkway
☎ 718/638-5000;
🕐 Wed–Fri 10–5, Sat–Sun 11–6 🚇 2, 3, Eastern Parkway-Brooklyn Museum

Prospect Park
➕ Off map to southeast
☎ 718/965-8999 🚇 2, 3 Grand Army Plaza Station; F 15th Street–Prospect Park

Brooklyn Children's Museum
www.brooklynkids.org
➕ Off map to southeast
✉ 145 Brooklyn Avenue, Crown Heights ☎ 718/735-4400 🕐 Opening hours vary, check website
🚇 C Kingston-Throop avenues ♿ Moderate

---

are the best Egyptian rooms outside the British Museum (and Egypt). With its grand entrance, it abuts Prospect Park—opened in 1867. The Botanic Garden, zoo and the Bandshell summertime events are highlights.

The bridge and beyond With its twin Gothic towers and ballet of cables, the first Manhattan–Brooklyn link fulfills beautifully its symbolic role of affording entry into new worlds of opportunity, and the view from here is spectacular. Worth exploring are the established brownstone neighborhoods of Park Slope, Cobble Hill and Brooklyn Heights, the latter famous for the Promenade and its view of Manhattan. Brooklyn Children's Museum, the world's first for kids, has tons to do, including a miniature theater and the "Totally Tots" toddler stamping ground.

More to See

BRONX ZOO

www.bronxzoo.com

The biggest city zoo in the US, 100 years old in 1999, has 4,000 animals, a kid's zoo and monorail. Don't miss the $43 million Congo Gorilla Forest.

✚ Off map to northeast ✉ Fordham Road (Bronx River Parkway Northeast) ☎ 718/367-1010 🕐 Apr–Oct daily 10–5; Nov–Mar 10–4.30 🍴 Restaurant 🚊 2, 5 West Farms Square–East Tremont Avenue ✋ Expensive

THE CLOISTERS

www.metmuseum.org

A 12th-century Spanish apse attached to a Romanesque cloister and a Gothic chapel—what's all this doing in the Bronx? This is the Met's medieval branch: The incongruity is hallucinogenic and the sights are just heavenly. The collections are arranged chronologically, so you can trace the metamorphosis of architectural styles. The bulk of the art and architecture was amassed by sculptor George Gray Bernard in the early 20th century. Much was rescued from ruin: The effigy of the Crusader Jean d'Alluye, for instance, was doing duty as a bridge, while the priceless Unicorn Tapestries were acting as frost blankets.

✚ Off map to north ✉ Fort Tryon Park, North Manhattan ☎ 212/923-3700 🕐 Mar–Oct Tue–Sun 9.30–5.15; Nov–Feb Tue–Sun 9.30–4.45; closed holidays 🚊 A 190th Street ✋ Expensive

CONEY ISLAND

www.coneyisland.com

At the end of the 19th century, Coney Island on a peak day played host to a million people. By 1921 a boardwalk and the subway had arrived, then 1939–40 added the "Parachute Jump," now a rusted ghost. The glory days of Luna Park are long since gone, yet seedy Coney Island still draws a crowd. The big-dipper ride, the Cyclone, is still there and Nathan's Famous hot dogs are still sold from the original site. A newer attraction is KeySpan Park, home of the Brookyn Cyclones baseball team. Look out for concerts held here in summer. The New York Aquarium moved here in

The restful garden at The Cloisters

A Kodiak bear at Bronx Zoo

1957 and roughly 10,000 creatures call it home, including beluga whales.
🚼 Off map to south ✉ Surf Avenue, Boardwalk; Aquarium: W 8th Street, Surf Avenue ☎ Sideshow 718/372-5159; KeySpan Park 718/449-8497; Aquarium 718/265-3474 🕐 Aquarium daily 10–5, summer weekends and holidays 10–7 🍴 Cafeteria at Aquarium 🚇 D, F, N Q Coney Island-Stillwell Avenue 👋 Aquarium expensive

QUEENS
The major attractions here are the New York Hall of Science and Queens Museum of Art, both at Flushing Meadows-Corona Park. The former is a hands-on science and technology museum with a great Science Playground outside for children (111th Street; tel 718/760-6565). The Queens Museum of Art (New York Building; tel 718/592-9700; www.queensmuseum.org) holds exhibitions of contemporary art, Tiffany glassware and a scale panorama of New York. Outside stands the Unisphere—the world's largest globe.
🚼 Off map to east

STATEN ISLAND
Fine historic sights are housed here. The Alice Austen House (2 Hylan Boulevard 718/816-4506; www.aliceausten.org) is a museum of photographs by Alice Austen in her Victorian house. Historic Richmond Town (441 Clarke Avenue; tel 718/351-1611; www.historicrichmondtown.org) is a restored rural village recreating the early 19th century.
🚼 Off map to southwest

YANKEE STADIUM
www.yankees.mlb.com
If you want to see what makes the New Yorker tick, go see a Yankees home game. The Yankees dominated the early era of baseball. In 1920 Babe Ruth joined the team and quickly became a hero. The team clinched the World Series title in 1996, 1998, 1999, and 2000.
🚼 Off map to north ✉ E 161st Street, Bronx ☎ 718/293-4300 🕐 Season runs Apr–Oct. Check schedule for games 🍴 Concession stands 🚇 4, B, D 161st Street-Yankee Stadium 👋 Expensive

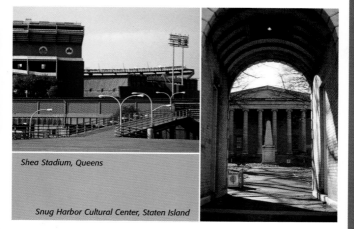

Shea Stadium, Queens

Snug Harbor Cultural Center, Staten Island

Restaurants

Prices are approximate, based on a 3-course meal for one person.
$$$ over $60
$$ $40–$60
$ under $40

BLUE RIBBON ($$)

There's a Manhattan feel to this deceptively huge modern-American favorite, and that's not surprising since it has an older sister there (97 Sullivan Street/ Prince Street), beloved by off-duty chefs. The comprehensive menu is perfectly balanced between creativity and comfort.
✉ 280 5th Avenue/1st Street, Brooklyn ☎ 718/840-0404
🚇 R Union Street

BUBBY'S ($)

www.bubbys.com
The DUMBO branch (down under Manhattan Bridge overpass) of this Tribeca favorite has an identical kitchen serving all-American BLTs, chicken clubs, meat loaf and fries followed by its divine pies but the rest differs enormously—operative word "enormous." Despite its size, expect a stroller jam and a wait at the door for Sunday brunch.
✉ 1 Main Street/Water Street, Brooklyn ☎ 718/222-0666
🚇 F York Street

GRIMALDI'S ($)

www.grimaldis.com
With one of the few remaining coal brick-ovens left in the city, Grimaldi's pizzas have assumed a legendary status. Dating back to 1905, "celeb" patrons have included Frank Sinatra and former Mayor Guiliani. Constant queues are testament to its enduring reputation.
✉ 19 Old Fulton Street, Brooklyn ☎ 718/858-4300
🚇 A, C High Street; 2 3 Clark Street

GROCERY ($$$)

A tiny place with a big reputation, this Carroll Gardens chef-owned place offers changing nouvelle-American menus. Inside is homey, but the lovely tree-shaded garden takes the cake.
✉ 288 Smith Street/Sacket, Brooklyn ☎ 718/596-3335
🚇 F, G Carroll Street

JUNIOR'S ($)

www.juniorscheesecake.com
An institution sited in a

SHERWOOD CAFÉ

It started out just selling funky French antiques, but the adjunct café grew until it took over entirely. One of the places that kicked the Brooklyn boom into high gear, the place is always packed, for the good French bistro food, the wacky interior and the fairy-tale graveled garden.
✉ 195 Smith Street/ Baltic Street, Brooklyn
☎ 718/596-1609
🚇 F, G Bergen Street

hideous stretch of downtown Brooklyn, this two-room diner is famous for its twin, two-roll, sandwiches and huge portions but, above all, for its delicious creamy, classic New York cheesecake.
✉ 386 Flatbush Avenue/ DeKalb Avenue, Brooklyn
☎ 718/852-5257 🚇 B, Q, R DeKalb Avenue

PETER LUGER ($$$)

www.peterluger.com
You get steak, some hash browns and creamed spinach for the table, and maybe some tomato-and-onion salad to start—that's it, and that's all you need. It's not about atmosphere or fine wines, it's not about feeling special, it's about steak. Since 1887 this landmark has been serving the best beef in New York.
✉ 178 Broadway/Driggs Avenue, Brooklyn ☎ 718/387-7400; no credit cards 🚇 J, Z Marcy Avenue

RIVER CAFÉ ($$$)

www.rivercafe.com
For a seriously special occasion and drop-dead views across the East River to Manhattan, this is a treat. Fine food, great service and a real touch of elegance. It does display slight pretentions (jackets required guys) but then we did say "special occasion."
✉ 1 Water Street, Brooklyn
☎ 718/522-5200 🚇 A, C High Street; 2, 3 Clark Street

You can pay a small fortune for little more than a shoebox in New York but with some research there are bargains to be had. Some hotels offer "free night" deals (such as buy three and get the fourth night free). So do shop around!

Introduction   **110**

Budget Hotels   **111**

Mid-Range Hotels   **112–113**

Luxury Hotels   **114**

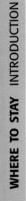

Introduction

There are plenty of hotel rooms but it is hard to find a comfortable room under $150. If money is no object, reserve a room at the Four Seasons.

On a Budget
For less expensive options, check out the inexpensive chains—Red Roof, Super 8 and others. The city also has some B&Bs, less expensive than the average hotel, with good-value extras. Hostels are the least expensive lodging options (▷ panel, below).

Luxury Living
You'll find first-class luxury hotels spread throughout the city, although many are centered in Midtown. Nearly every hotel room comes with air-conditioning, private bathroom, cable TV, telephone, coffeemaker, hand hair dryer, but top-class hotel rooms boast luxe fabrics and linens, high-tech electronics and high staff-to-guest ratios.

Prices
Today there is no such thing as a standard rack rate. Prices fluctuate with customer demand. To get the best rate on a hotel room, call the hotel and ask about the best available rate and special discounts. Alternatively, go online to such discount services as hotels.com, quikbook.com or hoteldiscounts.com. Note that taxes will be added to your bill, plus $2 occupancy tax on a standard room and 5.8 percent of the bill.

HOSTELS IN NEW YORK

Big Apple Hostel 119 W 45th, tel 212/302-2603.
Chelsea Center East 83 Essex Street, tel 212/260-0961
Chelsea International Hostel 251 W 20th Street, tel 212/647-0010.
Hostelling International 891 Amsterdam Avenue at W 103rd Street, tel 212/932-2300.
West Side YMCA 5 W 63rd Street, tel 212/875-4100.
Whitehouse 340 Bowery, tel 212/477-5623.

Top to bottom: arriving at the hotel; Peninsula Hotel; doorman at the Ritz-Carlton; Bryant Park hotel

Budget Hotels

PRICES

Expect to pay between $80 and $200 for a budget hotel

AMERITANIA HOTEL

www.ameritaniahotelnewyork.com
If you want to be in the heart of the theater district and a short walk from Times Square then the Ameritania provides mid-class accommodation with the added benefit of spacious common areas and lounge bar.

C10 ✉ 230 W 54th Street. ☎ 407/740-6442 🚇 D 55th Street; N, Q, R 57th Street-7th Avenue

BEDFORD HOTEL

www.bedfordhotel.com
There is a slightly dated feel to this midtown property, but for a great location and spacious rooms (by NY standards anyway) the Bedford is an excellent choice.

F12 ✉ 118 E 40th Street ☎ 212/221-6881 🚇 B, D, F, M 42nd Street-Bryant Square; 4, 5, 6, 7, 42nd Street–Grand Central

CARLTON ARMS

www.carltonarms.com
Decorated with crazy murals, this is perhaps New York's wackiest hotel. Amenities are minimal but there is a communal atmosphere that makes travelers feel at home. As it says on the business card, "this ain't no Holiday Inn."

The 54 comfortable rooms offer good-value accommodation.

F14 ✉ 160 E 25th Street/Lexington–3rd avenues ☎ 212/679-0680 🚇 6 23rd Street

HOTEL BELLECLAIRE

www.hotelbelleclaire.com
Mark Twain lived here, as did Maxim Gorky. Now the early-20th-century building offers 167 clean, minimal guest rooms, with pine furniture and pale apricot-color walls though only the shared-bathroom rooms are budget rate.

B6 ✉ 250 W 77th Street/Broadway–11th Avenue ☎ 212/362-7700 🚇 1 79th Street

HOTEL 17

www.hotel17ny.com
The kitschy decor almost looks deliberate—its stripey wallpaper, floral bedspread, nylon carpet look

seems to hit a chord with rock 'n' roll types and models. That could also be on account of its brownstone New York Gramercy Park location and its dirt cheap rates. Shared and private baths.

F15 ✉ 225 E 17th Street/2nd–3rd avenues ☎ 212/475-2845 🚇 L 3rd Avenue

HOTEL WOLCOTT

www.wolcott.com
Within walking distance of Macy's, the Empire State Building and other attractions, this hotel is great value for money. It has comfortable rooms with private bath and even offers free morning coffee and muffins.

D13 ✉ 4 W 31st Street, between 5th Avenue and Broadway ☎ 212/268-2900 🚇 B, D, F, M, N, Q, R 34th Street-Herald Square

WASHINGTON SQUARE

www.washingtonsquarehotel.com
This is the only hotel in the heart of Greenwich Village. Amenities are minimal—deliberately so, to keep the rates down—but the place still manages to be almost chic. 165 rooms.

E16 ✉ 103 Waverley Place/MacDougal Street ☎ 212/777-9515 🍴 Washington Square Restaurant 🚇 A, C, E, B, D, F, M 4th Street-Washington Square

B&BS

Those who prefer real neighborhoods, authentic experiences and behaving like a local may opt for a B&B. Often these are found in Brooklyn brownstones, where the host has an extra room. Others are empty apartments. The only imperative is to reserve ahead. Another ever-more-popular option is to check the sublet vacation rentals and housing swap listings at www.craigslist.org

Mid-Range Hotels

PRICES

Expect to pay between $200 and $400 for a mid-range hotel

70 PARK AVENUE

www.70parkave.com
The first foray into New York by boutique hotel pioneers Kimpton, this 205-room Murray Hill place has a quietly contemporary decor, extras like touch-screen room service, pillow menu, good sound systems and a special yoga channel on the huge flatscreen TV.
➕ E12 ✉ 70 Park Avenue/ 38th Street ☎ 212/973-2400 🍴 Silverleaf Tavern 🚇 4, 5, 6, 7, S Grand Central Station 42nd Street

BEEKMAN TOWER

www.thebeekmanhotel.com
The art deco tower in far-east Midtown has a lot going for it: well-kept rooms and suites, some with kitchens, most larger than the average with somewhat fusty but comfy furnishings, a fitness center, room service and two restaurants including the 26th-story Top of the Tower, with great river and city views.
➕ G10 ✉ 3 Mitchell Place/ 1st Avenue ☎ 212/355-7300 🚇 6 51st Street

COSMOPOLITAN

www.cosmohotel.com
No frills in any sense of the word exist at this 125-room, seven-story block in Tribeca. But, if you find the real estate rule applies to hotels, you'll love it—the location, location, location is prime. The clean, fully functional rooms vary a good deal in size, so if they're not full and you're not happy, ask to see another.
➕ E20 ✉ 95 W Broadway/ Chambers Street ☎ 212/566-1900 🚇 A, C Chambers Street

EXCELSIOR

www.excelsiorhotelny.com
The location is quite fabulous, steps from Central Park and the American Museum of Natural History, with the subway practically underfoot. The building is grand, too, heavy on the wood paneling, faux-oils and gilt frames. Rooms, though not beautiful in the generic brocades and stripes, are fine; some standard ones even overlook the park.
➕ C6 ✉ 45 W 81st Street/ Central Park West ☎ 212/ 362-9200 🚇 B, C 81st Street-Museum of Natural History

HOTEL BEACON

www.beaconhotel.com
In the middle of Broadway, on the Upper West Side, the Beacon feels more like an apartment building than a hotel. Some of the 200-plus rooms have kitchenettes.
➕ B7 ✉ 2130 Broadway/ 75th Street ☎ 212/787-1100 🚇 1, 2, 3 72nd Street

THE HUDSON

www.hudsonhotel.com
This place is all subdued lighting, trendy staff and minimalist chic but you're a short hop from Central Park (anyone for an early morning run?) and a Subway stop with great connections. The Hudson comes alive at night with a trendy bar and also boasts a reasonably equipped basement gym. Request a room (tiny, even by NY standards) overlooking the atrium as these tend to be quieter.
➕ B9 ✉ 356 W 58th Street. ☎ 212/554-6000 🚇 1, A, B, C, D 59th Street-Columbus Circle

JOLLY MADISON HOTEL

www.jollymadison.con
This is a very charming

THE ALGONQUIN

The Algonquin is forever associated with the only group of literary wits to be named after a piece of furniture: the Algonquin Round Table. The bon viveurs achieved almost as much at the bar here as they did in the pages of the embryo New Yorker, with Robert Benchley, Dorothy Parker and Alexander Woolcott well ensconced. The hotel's Rose Room still contains the very table they occupied.
www.algonquinhotel.com

Italian-run boutique hotel located on Madison Avenue. It has a warmth, elegance and style but what sets it apart is a blend of 1920s American architecture and modern facilities coupled with extremely comfortable and rather spacious rooms.

➕ E12 ✉ Madison Avenue at 38th Street ☎ 212/802-0600 🚇 B, D, F, M 42nd Street-Bryant Square

MARITIME HOTEL

www.themaritimehotel.com
Heat-seeking trendsters will love this quirky 120-room place in the thick of the Meatpacking District. Porthole windows facing the Hudson add a feature to the small rooms with a shiplike feel and navy-blue soft furnishings. Fitness center, happening bar scene and Japanese restaurant.

➕ C15 ✉ 363 W 16th Street/9th Avenue ☎ 212/242-4300 🍴 Matsuri 🚇 A, C, E 14th Street

OFF SOHO SUITES

www.offsoho.com
Since this place opened just a few years ago, its very off-SoHo location on the Lower East Side bordering Nolita has become all the rage. The suites are mini-studio apartments with no decorative advantages whatsoever but with full kitchens, private phones and satellite TV. The "Economy" suites share

kitchen and bathroom.
➕ F18 ✉ 11 Rivington Street/Bowery ☎ 212/979-9815 🚇 F Lower East Side-2nd Avenue; J, Z Bowery

THE SALISBURY

www.nycsalisbury.com
Across from Carnegie Hall and a short walk to Central Park and Fifth Avenue shopping, the Salisbury is comfortable in price as well as accommodations. The 119 rooms and 85 suites are large and quiet and most have refrigerators and serving pantries.
➕ D9 ✉ 123 W 57th Street, between 6th and 7th avenues ☎ 212/246-1300 🚇 N, Q, R 57th Street-7th Avenue; F 57th Street

THE SHOREHAM

www.shorehamhotel.com
The sleek Shoreham Hotel, behind the

LIBRARY

Each floor of the hotel is dedicated to a subject category from the Dewey Decimal system and each room has a collection of art and books related to a sub-category. The interior is modern and minimalist. Amenities include multiline phones with high-speed internet access.
www.libraryhotel.com
➕ E11 ✉ 299 Madison Avenue/41st Street ☎ 212/983-4500 🚇 S, 4, 5 6 7 Grand Central-42nd Street

Museum of Modern Art, has 174 small but nice rooms and suites, with ultra-suede walls, diffused lighting and puffy white comforters on the beds. The choice rooms are in the back. Extras such as Aveda products, free round-the-clock cappuccino and espresso and a hotel-curated art gallery, plus high-end electronics (Bose Wave, plasma screens, XBox 360s) in the better rooms add good value.

➕ D10 ✉ 33 W 55th Street/5th–6th avenues ☎ 212/247-6700 🍴 La Caravelle 🚇 B, Q 57th Street

THE TIME

www.thetimenycom
Just off Times Square, the 164 rooms and 28 suites sport bold, primary colors. Choose a red, yellow or blue room and you'll find that color not only covering the bed and selected wall parts but also appearing in candy and scent form. A Bose radio and Molton Brown toiletries add value but can't make the small rooms grow any larger, though you can spread out a bit in the small gym and rather swank lounge and restaurant.

➕ C11 ✉ 224 W 49th Street/8th Avenue ☎ 212/246-5252 🚇 N, Q, R, S, 1, 2, 3, 7 Times Square-42nd Street

Luxury Hotels

60 THOMPSON

www.60thompson.com
Fashionista boutique hotel in SoHo with 100 contemporary rooms. Most bathrooms have only showers. The rooftop bar/lounge, A60, is ever so glamorous, as is the Thai restaurant, Kittichai, and the bar, Thom.
✚ D18 ✉ 60 Thompson Street/Broome ☎ 212/431-0200 🚇 A, C, E Canal Street

CROSBY STREET HOTEL

www.firmdale.com
This new kid on the block is from uber-cool hoteliers Firmdale. On a cobbled street in the heart of New York's vibrant SoHo, the 86 rooms and suites over 11 floors have full-length warehouse-style windows. The interior design by Kit Hemp is fresh and contemporary, and the hotel has a gym and cinema.
✚ E18 ✉ 79 Crosby Street ☎ 212/226-6400 🚇 4, 6 Spring Street-Lafayette Street

FOUR SEASONS

www.fourseasons.com
The grandiose I. M. Pei building makes a big first impression—all towering lobbies, marble and mezzanine lounges. And the rooms don't disappoint. In beiges and creams, they're big, with tons of closets, tubs that fill in no time and, in some, great views. Many consider this Manhattan's top hotel.
✚ E9 ✉ 57 E 57th Street, Park–Madison avenues ☎ 212/758-5700 🍴 57, L'Atelier de Joël Robuchon 🚇 F, Q 57th Street

HOTEL GANSEVOORT

www.hotelgansevoort.com
You see the illuminated glass tower for blocks. Fashion-obsessed young creatives consider this area style-central, and populate the stark rooms with their stone and sand colors and high-tech everything, and the Ono restaurant and its O Bar. Rooftop pool.
✚ C16 ✉ 18 9th Avenue/13th Street ☎ 212/206-6700 🚇 A, C, E 14th Street; L 8th Avenue

INN AT IRVING PLACE

www.innatirving.com
With just 12 guest rooms

and junior suites, this discreet hotel is set in two 1830s townhouses near Gramercy Park, with elegant decor and a romantic atmosphere.
✚ E15 ✉ 56 Irving Place ☎ 212/533-4600 🍴 Casa Mono 🚇 4, 5, 6, L, N, Q, R 14th Street-Union Square

MANDARIN ORIENTAL

www.mandarinoriental.com
This chain is known for its clean lines, its fabulous spas and service. The best of the 248 rooms and suites have lovely panoramic views across Central Park.
✚ C9 ✉ 80 Columbus Circle/60th Street ☎ 212/805-8800 🍴 Asiate 🚇 A, B, C, D, 1 59th Street-Columbus Circle

RITZ-CARLTON BATTERY PARK

www.ritzcarlton.com
This glass-sided tower has one thing no other hotel has: the harbor. Decor in the rooms-with-everything is pale and contemporary, and the service and facilities are exemplary.
✚ D23 ✉ 2 West Street/Battery Place ☎ 212/344-0800 🚇 1 South Ferry

ST. REGIS

www.stregis.com
Formal Louis XV style in the middle of Midtown. The service is discreet, and the 182 rooms and suites are plush.
✚ E9–E10 ✉ 2 E 55th Street/5th Avenue ☎ 212/753-4500 🚇 E, M 5th Avenue-53rd Street

Use this section to help you plan your visit to New York. We have suggested the best ways to get around the city and useful information for while you are there.

Planning Ahead   116–117

Getting There   118

Getting Around   119–120

Essential Facts   121–123

Timeline   124–125

Need to Know

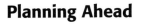

Planning Ahead

When to Go

Fall is generally thought the best time to visit New York. In August many New Yorkers are driven out of town by the searing heat. However, during this time lines are shorter, restaurant reservations optional and outdoor festivals at their peak. The city has occasional blizzards in winter, but these rarely cause disruption.

TIME

New York is on Eastern Standard Time, three hours ahead of Los Angeles and five hours behind the UK.

AVERAGE DAILY MAXIMUM TEMPERATURES

JAN	FEB	MAR	APR	MAY	JUN	JUL	AUG	SEP	OCT	NOV	DEC
39°F	41°F	46°F	61°F	70°F	81°F	84°F	82°F	77°F	66°F	54°F	39°F
4°C	5°C	8°C	16°C	21°C	27°C	29°C	28°C	25°C	19°C	12°C	4°C

Spring (March to May) is unpredictable—even in April snow showers can alternate with shirtsleeves weather—but the worst of winter is over by mid-March.
Summer (June to August) can be extremely hot and humid, especially July and August.
Fall (September to November) sees warm temperatures persisting into October.
Winter (December to February) can be severe, with heavy snow, biting winds and subfreezing temperatures.

WHAT'S ON

January/February
Chinese New Year (Chinatown).
Martin Luther King Day Parade (3rd Mon in Jan, 5th Avenue, 61st–86th streets).
March 17 *St. Patrick's Day Parade* (5th Avenue, 44th–86th streets).
March/April *Easter Parade* (5th Avenue, 44th–57th streets).
April–October *Baseball*
May *9th Avenue International Food Festival* (9th Avenue, 37th–57th streets ☎ 518/474-4116).
June *Metropolitan Opera park concerts* (☎ 212/362-6000).

Lesbian and Gay Pride Parade (52nd Street and 5th Avenue to Christopher and Greenwich streets).
July 4 *Independence Day*
June–September *Shakespeare in the Park* (Delacorte Theater ☎ 212/539-8655).
NY Philharmonic park concerts.
August *Harlem Week* (☎ 212/862-7200).
August–September *Lincoln Center Out-of-Doors Festival* (☎ 212/875-5000).
US Open Tennis Championships (☎ 718/760-6200).
September *Feast of San Gennaro* (Little Italy).

September–October *New York Film Festival* (Lincoln Center ☎ 212/875-5601).
Columbus Day Parade (5th Avenue, 44th–79th streets).
November *NYC Marathon* (Staten Island to Central Park; www.nycmarathon.org).
Macy's Thanksgiving Day Parade (✉ Central Park West, 77th Street ☎ 212/494-4495).
December *Tree Lighting Ceremony* (✉ Rockefeller Center ☎ 212/332-6868).
New Year's Eve celebrations (✉ Times Square).

New York City Online

www.ilovenytheater.com
Offers up-to-the-minute details on show times and tickets, as well as reviews.

http://newyork.citysearch.com
City Search has links to and listings for attractions, entertainment, restaurants, shopping, hotels and more. Also has news, reviews and a directory offering NYC information.

www.nyc.gov
As the official homepage of the City of New York, the site offers links to the Office of the Mayor as well as information about community services, legal policies, city agencies, news and weather and visitor information.

www.ny.com
Billing itself as "the paperless guide to New York City," ny.com's "How, Wow and Now" sections let you know what's up on New York's entertainment, dining and nightlife scene. The sports section lists professional events.

www.nygo.com
Trip planner and hotel booker of the NYC Information Center, which opened in Midtown in 2009.

www.nytimes.com
Here you'll get an inside look at one of the world's most respected newspapers. The site has links to sections covering everything from world affairs to sports and local gossip.

www.nycvisit.com
The official tourism website includes a calendar of events, accommodations information, updates on laws, transport and lots more.

www.timessquare.com
All about Times Square and the area around, Broadway and its theaters in particular, with booking information.

PRIME TRAVEL SITES

www.fodors.com
A complete travel-planning site. You can research prices and weather; book air tickets, cars and rooms; pose questions to fellow travelers and find links to other sites.

www.iloveny.com
Official NY State site. Information about touring the region.

www.mta.info
The Metropolitan Transportation Authority updates you on service changes and disruptions, and answers questions about buses and subway.

INTERNET ACCESS

Anywwwhere Internet Services have internet cafés locatied in cafés and restaurants across the city. For locations check http://anywwwhere.com

Kinko's have locations throughout the city, many open 24 hours.

Wireless internet is available at many places, including coffee shops, parks, libraries and some hotels.

Getting There

ENTRY REQUIREMENTS

Visitors to New York from outside the US must have a full passport and a return ticket. Visitors are required to obtain an electronic authorization to travel at least 72 hours prior to departure. Go to https://esta.cbp.dhs.gov to make an application. Leave plenty of time to clear security as the levels of checks are constantly being stepped up.

FROM LAGUARDIA

The journey to Manhattan takes between 45 and 60 minutes. SuperShuttle runs a shared minibus 24 hours (cost $13). Services to Manhattan are also provided by New York Airport Service Express (cost $12). Taxis cost $21–$30 to Manhattan, plus tolls and tip.

ARRIVING BY LAND

● Greyhound buses from across the US and Canada and commuter buses from New Jersey arrive at the Port Authority Terminal (✉ 625 8th Avenue ☎ 212/564-8484).
● Commuter trains use Grand Central Terminal (✉ 42nd Street/Park Avenue ☎ 212/532-4900).
● Long-distance trains arrive at Pennsylvania Station (✉ 31st Street/8th Avenue).

AIRPORTS

New York has three airports—John F. Kennedy (J.F.K.) (✉ Queens, 15 miles/24km east of Manhattan ☎ 718/244-4444), Newark (✉ New Jersey, 16 miles/25km west ☎ 973/961-6000) and LaGuardia (✉ Queens, 8 miles/13km east ☎ 718/533-3400). Most international flights arrive at J.F.K. For details, visit www.panynj.gov

18 MILES (29KM)

LaGuardia Airport
8 miles (13km) to city center. Bus/minibus 30–45 minutes, $12

Manhattan

Newark Liberty International Airport
16 miles (25km) to city center. Bus/minibus 40 minutes, $18

J.F.K. International Airport
15 miles (24km) to city center. Bus/minibus 1 hour, $15

FROM J.F.K.

The journey to Manhattan takes around an hour. New York Airport Service Express Bus (☎ 718/875-8200) runs every 20 minutes, 6.15am–11.10pm ($15). The SuperShuttle (☎ 800/258-3826) runs to Manhattan 24 hours a day ($18). To reserve, use the courtesy telephone next to the Ground Transportation Desk. A free shuttle bus runs to the A train. Taxis costs $45 plus tolls; use the official taxi stand. The AirTrain to Jamaica (E.J.Z. subway and Long Island Railroad) or Howard Beach (A subway) costs $5 and takes 12 minutes, plus 35–75 minutes to Midtown. It runs every 5–10 minutes, 24 hours a day.

FROM NEWARK

It takes about 60 minutes to Manhattan. AirTrain (☎ 888/397-4636) goes direct from all terminals 24 hours a day to Penn Station (A, C, E, 1, 2, 3 subway); follow signs to Monorail/AirTrain. SuperShuttle (☎ 800/258–3826) runs a minibus to Midtown 24 hours a day ($18). A taxi costs $50–$80, plus tolls and a $15 surcharge from Manhattan.

Getting Around

BUSES

● Bus stops are on or near corners, marked by a sign and a yellow painted curb. Any ride costs the same as the subway and you can use a Metrocard or correct change ($2–$25).

● Bus maps are available from token booth clerks in subway stations.

● Buses are safe, clean and excruciatingly slow. The fastest are Limited Stop buses.

● If you pay by Metrocard you may transfer free from bus–subway or bus–bus within two hours of the time you paid the fare.

● A bus map is essential.

SUBWAY

● At the time of going to press, several of New York's subway lines were changing. Please check the latest information before you travel. Transit information ☎ 718/330-1234
🕐 24 hours; www.mta.info

● New York's subway system has 24 routes and 468 stations, many open 24 hours (those with a green globe outside are always staffed).

● To ride the subway you need a Metrocard, which you can refill. Unlimited ride Metrocards are also available; with these you must wait 18 minutes between swipes. Swipe the card to enter the turnstile.

● Many stations have separate entrances for up- and downtown services. Make sure you take a local train, not a restricted-stop express.

● Children under 44in (113cm) tall ride free.

● Avoid the less populated subway lines at night. If you ride at night, stay in the "off hour waiting area" until your train arrives.

TAXIS

● The ubiquitous yellow cab is a New York trademark and, except possibly on very wet or busy evenings, very easy to hail. Hotel concierge can arrange and most bars, restaurants and nightspots will be able to assist. If you want to book something in advance try one of the companies in the panel (right).

● Cab drivers are notorious for (a) knowing

LOST PROPERTY

● You are unlikely to recover items but try the following (or call 311, city helpline):
Subway and bus
☎ 212/712-4500
Taxi
☎ 212/639-9675
J.F.K.
☎ 718/244-4225/6
Newark
☎ 973/961-6243
Report a loss quickly if claiming on your insurance.

SUBWAY TIPS

● If your Metrocard doesn't work, don't go to a different turnstile or you'll lose a fare. As the display says, you should "swipe again."

● Check the circular signs on the outside of the cars to make sure you're boarding the correct train. Often two lines share a platform.

● Look at the boards above your head to check whether you're on the Up- or Downtown side and/or on the Local or Express track.

TAXIS

123 24 Hour Taxi
☎ 212/239-0404
Carmel Car and Limousine
☎ 212/666-6666
Dial 7 Car and Limousine
☎ 212/777-7777

NEED TO KNOW GETTING AROUND

BROOKLYN

If you're visiting sights in Brooklyn, the same subway rules apply, but you may have to change trains as several local lines (1, 6, E, M) only operate in Manhattan (not Queens). The B51 bus runs between City Hall/Park Row in Manhattan and Smith/Fulton streets in Brooklyn on weekdays. It crosses Manhattan Bridge.

VISITORS WITH DISABILITIES

City law requires that all facilities constructed after 1987 provide complete access to people with disabilities. Many owners of older buildings have willingly added disability-access features as well. Two important resources are the Mayor's Office for People with Disabilities (✉ 100 Gold Street, 2nd floor, 10038 ☎ 212/788-2830; www.nyc.gov/mopd) and Hospital Audiences' guide to New York's cultural institutions, *Access for All* (☎ 212/575-7676; www.hospitalaudiences.org). This online guide describes the accessibility of each place, with information on hearing and visual aids, alternative entrances and the height of telephones and water fountains. H.A. also provides descriptions of theater performances for people with visual impairments.

nothing about New York geography, (b) not speaking English and (c) having an improvisational driving style.

● Tip at least 15 percent. Bills larger than $10 are unpopular for short journeys.

DRIVING

● Driving in New York is not recommended, but a car is essential for excursions farther afield.

● The address of the nearest major car-rental outlet can be found by calling the following toll-free numbers:

Avis ☎ 800/331-1212
Budget ☎ 800/527-0700
Hertz ☎ 800/654-3131
National ☎ 877/222-9058

● If driving in New York is unavoidable, make sure you understand the restrictions because penalties for infringements are stringent.

● In many streets parking alternates daily from one side to the other and it is illegal to park within 10ft (3m) either side of a fire hydrant. A car illegally parked will be towed away and the driver heavily fined.

● Within the city limits right turns at a red light are prohibited and the speed limit is 30mph (48kph).

● Passing a stopped school bus is illegal and stiff fines can be imposed.

WALKING

New York is one of the few US cities in which the predominant mode of transportation is walking. Especially if the weather is cooperating (and if it isn't, umbrella vendors materialize on every other corner), it's far nicer to hike a 10- or 20-block distance than to descend below ground on the subway, or sit in a cab stalled in traffic. It's also often faster. To work it out for yourself, figure one minute per short block (north–south) and two per long block (east–west, on cross streets). New Yorkers tend to walk fast and there are few collisions.

Essential Facts

CUSTOMS
● Non-US citizens may import duty-free: 1 quart (just under a liter) of alcohol (no one under 21 can import alcohol), 200 cigarettes or 50 cigars and $100 of gifts.
● Among restricted items for import are meat, fruit, plants, seeds and certain prescription medicines without a prescription or written statement from your doctor.

ELECTRICITY
● The supply is 100 volts, 60 cycles AC current.
● US appliances use flat two-prong plugs. European appliances require an adapter.

ETIQUETTE
● Tipping: waitstaff get 15–20 percent (roughly double the 8.875 percent sales tax at the bottom of the bill); so do cab drivers. Bartenders get about the same (though less than $1 is stingy). Bellhops ($1 per bag), room service waiters (10 percent), and hairdressers (15–20 percent) should also be tipped.
● There are stringent smoking laws in New York. Smoking is banned on all public transportation, in cabs and in all places of work, including restaurants and bars.

MEDICAL TREATMENT
● It is essential to have adequate insurance.
● In the event of an emergency, the 911 operator will send an ambulance.
● Doctors on Call (24 hours) ☎ 212/737-1212
● Near Midtown, 24-hour emergency rooms: Roosevelt Hospital ✉ 10th Avenue and 59th Street ☎ 212/523-4000
St. Vincent's Hospital ✉ 7th Avenue/12th Street ☎ 212/604-7000
● Dental Emergency Service ☎ 646/837-7806. An operator will put you in touch with a dentist close to you open 24/7.

VISITOR INFORMATION
● NYC & Company provides free bus and subway maps, calendars of events and discount coupons for Broadway shows ✉ 810 7th Avenue ☎ 212/484-1222; www.nyc go.com ⏰ Mon–Fri 8.30–6, weekends 9–5. There are also information booths at City Hall Park, Federal Hall, Chinatown and Harlem.
● Times Square Information Center provides free maps and brochures, sells tickets for transport and entertainment and has a restaurant reservation booth ✉ 1560 Broadway between 46th and 47th streets ☎ 212/768-1560; www.timessquarenyc.org ⏰ Mon–Fri 9–7, Sat–Sun 8–8

EMERGENCY NUMBERS
● Police, Fire Department, Ambulance ☎ 911
● Crime Victims Hotline ☎ 212/577-7777
● Sex Crimes Report Line ☎ 212/267-7273

TOILETS
● Almost every department store has facilities, as do many smaller stores and key visitor attractions. Hotel lobbies, bars and restaurants offer rest rooms. Do exercise caution in using facilities at public transportation hubs or in less salubrious neighborhoods.

MONEY

The unit of currency is the dollar (= 100 cents). Notes (bills) come in denominations of $1, $2, $5, $10, $20, $50 and $100; coins come in 25¢ (a quarter), 10¢ (a dime), 5¢ (a nickel) and 1¢ (a penny).

5 dollars

10 dollars

50 dollars

100 dollars

TRAVEL INSURANCE

Check your insurance policy and buy a supplementary policy if needed. A minimum of $1 million medical cover is recommended. Choose a policy that also includes trip cancellation, baggage and document loss.

MONEY MATTERS

● Credit cards are widely accepted. Visa, MasterCard, American Express, Diner's Card and Discover are most commonly used.
● US dollar traveler's checks are often accepted in lieu of cash. It is difficult to exchange foreign currency traveler's checks, even at banks, and fees are high.

NEWSPAPERS AND MAGAZINES

● The local papers are the *New York Times* (with a Sunday edition), the *Daily News* (also with Sunday supplements) and the *New York Post*. The free alternative paper the *Village Voice* has extensive listings. Also look for the respected *Wall Street Journal* and the pink-hued, gossip-heavy, weekly *New York Observer*.
● As well as the *New Yorker, New York* and *Time Out New York*, you may also see the hip *Paper*, the glossy *In New York* and *Where* magazines and the even glossier *Avenue*.

OPENING HOURS

● Banks: Mon–Fri 9–3 or 3.30; some are open longer, and on Saturday.
● Stores: Mon–Sat 10–6; many are open far later, and on Sunday 12–6; those in the Villages, Nolita and SoHo open and close later.
● Museums: hours vary, but Monday is the most common closing day.
● Post offices: Mon–Fri 8 or 9–6. Some open Sat 9–4.
● Opening times given are for general guidance only.

MAIL AND TELEPHONES

● The main post office ✉ 8th Avenue (33rd Street) ☎ 212/330-3002 is open 24 hours. Branch post offices are listed in Yellow Pages.
● Stamps are also available from hotel concierges, online at www.usps.com, at some delis and from vending machines in stores.
● All New York numbers require the prefix to be dialed (212, 718, 646, 347 or 917). For long-distance calls, add a "1" before the code.

● Hotels can levy hefty surcharges so best to use payphones or the prepaid international phone cards.

● Watch out for mobile roaming charges that can result in an unwanted bill on return home; ask your mobile provider for "bolt-on" packages for use while in New York (especially if you are planning on receiving emails, using the web or downloading information).

● To call the US from the UK, dial 001. To call the UK from the US, dial 011 44, then drop the first zero from the area code.

SENSIBLE PRECAUTIONS

● Maintain awareness of your surroundings and of other people, and try to look as though you know your way around.

● Don't get involved with street crazies, however entertaining they are.

● The less populated subway lines are best avoided at night and also certain areas of Brooklyn. Generally, areas of Manhattan that were once considered unsafe (Alphabet City east of Avenue C, the far west of Midtown, north of about 110th Street and Central Park) are far less edgy than they used to be. Still, keep your wits about you in deserted areas.

● Use common-sense rules: conceal your wallet; keep the fastener of your bag on the inside; and don't flash large amounts of cash or jewelry.

RADIO AND TELEVISION

● NY1 is the main channel serving the New York boroughs and will give you access to news, weather and travel as well as its own take on daily life in the Big Apple.

● WNYC (New York Public Radio) on 93.0 FM and 820 AM is also a good bet for news, culture and music.

● Catch a television show recording? Tickets for The Late Show with David Letterman are available at www.cbs.com/late_night/late_show/tickets/

STUDENTS

● An International Student Identity Card (ISIC) is good for reduced admission at many museums, theaters and other attractions.

● Carry the ISIC or some other photo ID card at all times, to prove you're a full-time student or over 21.

● Under-25s will find it expensive to rent a car.

NEED TO KNOW ESSENTIAL FACTS

CONSULATES		
Australia	✉ 150 E 4nd Street	☎ 212/351-6500
Canada	✉ 1251 6th Avenue	☎ 212/596-1628
Denmark	✉ 885 2nd Avenue, 18th Floor	☎ 212/223-4545
France	✉ 934 5th Avenue	☎ 212/606-3600
Germany	✉ 871 UN Plaza	☎ 212/610-9700
Ireland	✉ 345 Park Avenue	☎ 212/319-2555
Italy	✉ 690 Park Avenue	☎ 212/737-9100
Netherlands	✉ 1 Rockefeller Plaza	☎ 877/388-2443
Norway	✉ 825 3rd Avenue	☎ 212/421-7333
UK	✉ 845 3rd Avenue	☎ 212/745-0200

Timeline

Pre-1600 New York is populated by Native American groups.

1609 Henry Hudson sails up the Hudson seeking the Northwest Passage.

1625 "Nieuw Amsterdam" is founded by the Dutch West India Company. A year later the colony's leader buys Manhattan Island from the Native Americans for $24 of trinkets.

1664 The British invade.

1776 American Revolutionary War begins.

1783 War ends. Two years later New York becomes capital of the United States.

1789 George Washington is sworn in as first US president at Federal Hall.

1790 Philadelphia becomes US capital.

1807 Robert Fulton launches his first steamboat, creating trade routes that make many New Yorkers' fortunes.

1827 Slavery in New York is abolished.

1848 Start of first great immigrant waves.

1861 New York backs the Union during the Civil War.

1868 The first "El" (elevated train) opens.

1886 The Statue of Liberty is unveiled.

1892 Ellis Island opens.

1904 New York's first subway opens.

1929 The Great Depression begins.

1933 Prohibition ends. Fiorello LaGuardia becomes mayor.

1954 Ellis Island is closed down.

1964 Race riots in Harlem and Brooklyn.

1975 A federal loan saves New York City from bankruptcy.

1990 David Dinkins, New York's first black mayor, takes office.

2001 Terrorists fly two hijacked planes into the WTC twin towers, killing an estimated 3,000 people in the 9/11 tragedy.

2002 Rudy Giuliani's term as mayor ends. Michael Bloomberg takes office.

2004 New Yorkers vote overwhelmingly for presidential candidate John Kerry. President George W. Bush begins second term.

2009 Former New York Senator Hillary Clinton becomes Secretary of State under Democratic President Barack Obama.

TENEMENT LIFE

As you make your first explorations in New York, consider how it was for the early immigrants, especially those who were herded through Ellis Island, then crammed into Lower East Side tenements. Imagine how daunting the cast iron-framed SoHo buildings must have appeared to someone from, say, Vienna. Although they are now the scene of costly loft living, or home to chain stores or swank boutiques, during the immigrant boom they were sweatshop skyscrapers–symbols of hope for a fresh future. (See Lower East Side Tenement Museum ▷ 29.)

Left to right: an early view of the Bay of New York; Customs House, New York; Brooklyn Bridge in the 19th century; modern-day transportation on the subway

Index

A

Abby Aldrich Rockefeller Sculpture Garden 60
accommodations 109–114
  B&B 110, 111
  hostels 110
  hotels 17, 110, 111–114
airports 118
Algonquin, The 112
Alice Austen House 107
American Museum of Natural History 8, 92–93
Arch, The 43
art galleries, commercial 42
Asia Society 84
Avery Fisher Hall 95, 99

B

B&B 110, 111
banks 122
bars 13
see also entertainment and nightlife
baseball 18, 106, 107
Battery Park 29
Block Beautiful 42
book stores 12, 85, 97
Botanic Garden 105
Broadway 63
Bronx Zoo 17, 106
Brooklyn 4, 5, 8, 104–105, 120
Brooklyn Children's Museum 105
Brooklyn Museum of Art 104–105
buses 119

C

cabaret 46, 86
car rental 120
Carnegie Hall 69
celebrity sightings 13
Central Park 6, 8, 18, 74–75, 86
children's entertainment 17
Children's Museum of the Arts 29
Chinatown 8, 24
Christopher Park 44
Chrysler Building 6, 8, 52–53
cinemas 99
City Hall 29
City Pass 79
climate and seasons 116
Cloisters, The 106
clubs 13, 69
see also entertainment and nightlife

cocktail culture 33
comedy clubs 13, 18, 46, 69, 99
concert venues 69, 86, 95, 99
Coney Island 106–107
consulates 123
Cooper-Hewitt Design Museum 8, 76
Cooper Union 38
credit cards 122
customs regulations 121

D

David H Koch Theater 95
dental services 121
department stores 12, 17
disabilities, visitors with 120
Downtown 35–48
  entertainment and nightlife 46
  map 36–37
  restaurants 48
  shopping 45
  sights 38–43
  walk 44
driving 120
drugstores 121

E

East Village 8, 38–39
eating out 14–15, 16, 18
  see also restaurants
electricity 121
Ellis Island 7, 8, 25
emergency telephone numbers 121
Empire State Building 8, 54–55
entertainment and nightlife 13, 16
  Downtown 46
  listings 33, 117
  Lower Manhattan 33
  Midtown 69
  Upper East Side and Central Park 86
  Upper West Side 99
etiquette 121
events and festivals 116

F

FAO Schwarz 17, 68
fashion shopping 10, 11, 12, 32, 45, 68, 85, 97
Fifth Avenue 6, 8, 31, 56–57
Flatiron Building 42
flea markets 11
food and drink
  bagels 45
  brunch 100

  eating out 14–15, 16, 18
  shopping for 12, 32
  street food 11
  see also restaurants
Freedom Tower 5, 29
free entertainment 97
Frick Collection 8, 77

G

Grace Church 39, 42–43
Gracie Mansion 84
Gramercy Park 43
Grand Central Terminal 6, 8, 58–59, 70
Greenmarket 41, 45
Greenwich Village 8, 31, 40
Greyhound buses 118
Ground Zero 29
Guggenheim Museum 7, 8, 78–79

H

Haughwout Building 30
history 124–125
homewares stores 12, 45, 85
hostels 110
hotels 17, 110, 111–114

I

insurance 122
International Center of Photography 6, 65
Internet cafés 117
itineraries 6–7

J

Jefferson Market Library 40, 44
Jewish Museum 84
Juilliard School of Music 95

L

Lincoln Center 7, 8, 94–95
"Lipstick Building" 65
lost property 119
Lower East Side Tenement Museum 29
Lower Manhattan 20–34
  entertainment and nightlife 33
  map 22–23
  restaurants 34
  shopping 32
  sights 24–30
  walk 31

M

Macy's 68
Madison Avenue 63
Madison Square Garden 18, 65, 67, 69

maps
Downtown 36–37
Lower Manhattan 22–23
Midtown 50–51
New York farther afield
102–103
Upper East Side and
Central Park 72–73
Upper West Side 90–91
markets 41
Meatpacking District 43, 44
medical treatment 121
Metropolitan Museum of Art
7, 8, 80–81
Metropolitan Opera House
95, 99
Midtown 49–70
entertainment and nightlife
69
map 50–51
restaurants 70
shopping 68
sights 52–66
walk 67
MoMA (Museum of Modern
Art) 6, 8, 60
money 122
Morgan Library 65
Museo del Barrio 84
Museum of the City of New
York 84
museum opening hours 122
music stores 10–11

N
narrowest house in NYC 40
National Arts Club 43
Neue Galerie New York 7, 84
New Museum of
Contemporary Art 29
New York Aquarium 106–107
New York City Police
Museum 30
New York farther afield
101–108
map 102–103
restaurants 108
sights 104–107
New York Hall of Science 107
New York Public Library 8, 61
New York Stock Exchange 30
newspapers and magazines
122

O
opening hours 122
opera 95, 99

P
Paley Center for Media 66

parking 120
passports and visas 118
Pearl River Mart 32
police 121
post offices and postal
services 122
Prospect Park 105
public transportation 119–120

Q
Queens 107
Queens Museum of Art 107

R
Radio City Music Hall 62, 69
radio and television 123
restaurants 14, 15, 16, 18
Downtown 48
Lower Manhattan 34
Midtown 70
New York farther afield 108
Upper East Side and
Central Park 88
Upper West Side 100
Richmond Town 107
river cruises 13
Rockefeller Center 6, 8, 62,
67
Rose Center 92
The Row 43

S
safety, personal 4, 123
St. Marks-in-the-Bowery 43
St. Patrick's Cathedral 66
St. Patrick's Old Cathedral 30
sales tax 14
sample sales 11, 85
Seaport Museum Visitors'
Center 28
shopping 10–12, 56–57
Downtown 45
Lower Manhattan 32
Midtown 68
opening hours 122
Upper East Side and
Central Park 85
Upper West Side 97
shopping spree 8, 63
Singer Building 30
smoking etiquette 121
SoHo Cast Iron Historic
District 30, 31
South Street Seaport 8, 28
sports 18
Staten Island 107
Statue of Liberty 7, 8, 26–27
Stonewall Inn 40
Strawberry Fields 75, 96
student travelers 123

Stuyvesant-Fish House 39
subway system 119

T
taxis 119–120
telephones 122–123
tenements 125
theaters 69, 86, 95, 99
ticket outlets 64
time differences 116
Times Square 6, 8, 64
tipping 14, 120, 121
toilets 121
Tompkins Square Park 38
Top of the Rock 62
train services 118
travel arrangements 117, 118
traveler's checks 122
Trump Tower 66

U
Ukrainian Museum 39
Union Square 8, 41
United Nations Headquarters
66
Upper East Side and Central
Park 71–88
entertainment and nightlife
86
map 72–73
restaurants 88
shopping 85
sights 74–84
Upper West Side 89–100
entertainment and nightlife
99
map 90–91
restaurants 100
shopping 97
sights 92–95
walk 96

V
visitor information 117, 121

W
walking in New York 120
walks
Downtown 44
Lower Manhattan 31
Midtown 67
Upper West Side 96
Washington Square 43, 44
websites 117
Whitney Museum of
American Art 8, 82–83
Woolworth Building 30

Y
Yankee Stadium 107

New York City's
25 BEST

WRITTEN BY Kate Sekules
UPDATED BY David Leck
DESIGN WORK Jacqueline Bailey
COVER DESIGN Tigist Getachew
INDEXER Marie Lorimer
IMAGE RETOUCHING AND REPRO Sarah Montgomery and James Tims
REVIEWING EDITOR Linda Schmidt
PROJECT EDITOR Apostrophe S Limited
SERIES EDITOR Marie-Claire Jefferies

ISBN 978-1-4000-0545-1

NINTH EDITION

IMPORTANT TIP
Time inevitably brings changes, so always confirm prices, travel facts, and other perishable information when it matters. Although Fodor's cannot accept responsibility for errors, you can use this guide in the confidence that we have taken every care to ensure its accuracy.

SPECIAL SALES
This book is available for special discounts for bulk purchases for sales promotions or premiums. Special editions, including personalized covers, excerpts of existing books, and corporate imprints, can be created in large quantities for special needs. For more information, write to Special Markets/Premium Sales, 1745 Broadway, MD 6–2, New York, NY 10019 or email specialmarkets@randomhouse.com.

Color separation by AA Digital Department
Printed and bound by Leo Paper Products, China
10 9 8 7 6 5 4 3 2 1

A04202
Maps in this title produced from map data © Tele Atlas N.V. 2010   Tele Atlas
Transport map © Communicarta Ltd, UK

The Automobile Association would like to thank the following photographers, companies and picture libraries for their assistance in the preparation of this book.

Abbreviations for the picture credits are as follows – (t) top; (b) bottom; (c) centre; (l) left; (r) right; (AA) AA World Travel Library.

1 AA/J Tims; **2/3t** AA/C Sawyer; **4/5t** AA/C Sawyer; **4tl** AA/C Sawyer; **5** AA/C Sawyer; **6/7t** AA/C Sawyer; **6cl** AA/S McBride; **6c** AA/C Sawyer; **6cr** AA/C Sawyer; **6bl** AA/S McBride; **6br** AA/S McBride; **7cl** AA/C Sawyer; **7c** AA/C Sawyer; **7cr** AA/C Sawyer; **7bl** AA/C Sawyer; **7bc** AA/D Corrance; **7br** AA/C Sawyer; **8/9t** AA/C Sawyer; **10/11** AA/C Sawyer; **10t** AA/C Sawyer; **10c** AA/C Sawyer; **10b** AA/ M Jourdan; **11tl** AA/ C Sawyer; **11ctl** AA/S McBride; **11c** AA/C Sawyer; **11cbl** AA/C Sawyer; **11bl** AA/C Sawyer; **12/13t** AA/C Sawyer; **12b** AA/C Sawyer; **13tl** AA/C Sawyer; **13ctl** AA/C Sawyer; **13c** Photodisc; **13cbl** Brand X pics; **13bl** AA/C Sawyer; **14/5t** AA/C Sawyer; **14tr** AA/C Sawyer; **14tcr** AA/P Kenward; **14c** AA/C Sawyer; **14bcr** AA/C Sawyer;**14br** AA/S McBride; **15b** AA/S McBride; **16/7t** AA/C Sawyer; **16t** Photodisc; **16c** AA/R Elliot; **16b** AA/C Sawyer; **17t** AA/S McBride; **17tc** AA/S McBride; **17bc** AA; **17b** AA/C Sawyer; **18t** AA/C Sawyer; **18tc** AA/R Elliot; **18c** AA/D Corrance; **18cb** AA/P Kenward; **18b** AA/S Collier; **19(I)** AA/C Sawyer; **19(II)** AA/S McBride; **19(III)** AA/C Sawyer; **19(IV)** AA/C Sawyer; **19(V)** AA/C Sawyer; **19(VI)** AA/C Sawyer; **20/1** AA/S McBride; **24tl** AA/C Sawyer; **24tr** AA/C Sawyer; **25tl** AA/C Sawyer; **25tr** AA/S McBride; **26l** AA/C Sawyer; **26/7t** AA/R Elliot; **26/7b**; AA/C Sawyer; **27r** AA/C Sawyer; **28l** AA/C Sawyer; **28r** AA/C Sawyer; **29t** AA/C Sawyer; **29bl** AA/C Sawyer; **29br** AA/C Sawyer; **30t** AA/C Sawyer; **30bl** AA/C Sawyer; **30br** AA/C Sawyer; **31t** AA/C Sawyer; **32t** AA/C Sawyer; **33t** AA/S McBride; **34t** AA/C Sawyer; **35** AA/C Sawyer; **38tl** AA/S McBride; **38bl** AA/C Sawyer; **38/9t** AA/S McBride; **38br** AA/C Sawyer; **38/9br** AA/C Sawyer; **39r** AA/C Sawyer; **40tl** AA/S McBride; **40tc** AA/S McBride; **40tr** AA/S McBride; **41tl** AA/C Sawyer; **41tr** AA/C Sawyer; **42/3t** AA/C Sawyer; **42bl** AA/C Sawyer; **42br** AA/C Sawyer; **43bl** AA/C Sawyer; **43br** AA/C Sawyer; **44t** AA/C Sawyer; **45t** AA/C Sawyer; **46t** Digitalvision; **47** AA/S McBride; **48t** AA/C Sawyer; **49** AA/C Sawyer; **52tl** AA/C Sawyer; **52/3t** AA/S McBride; **53tr** AA/R Elliot; **54tl** AA/S McBride; **54/5t** AA/R Elliot; **54br** AA/D Corrance; **54/5b** AA/C Sawyer; **55r** AA/C Sawyer; **56** AA/C Sawyer; **56/7** AA/C Sawyer; **58/9** AA/S McBride; **59t** AA/S McBride; **59bl** AA/S McBride; **59br** AA/S McBride; **60tl** 2010 Timothy Hursley/MOMA; **60tc** 2010 Timothy Hursley/MOMA; **60tr** 2010 Timothy Hursley/MOMA; **61tl** AA/R Elliot; **61tr** AA; **62tl** AA/C Sawyer; **62tc** AA/C Sawyer; **62tr** AA/C Sawyer; **63tl** AA/C Sawyer; **63tr** AA/C Sawyer; **64tl** AA/S McBride; **64tr** AA/C Sawyer; **65t** AA/C Sawyer; **65b** Norman McGrath/ International Center of Photography; **66t** AA/C Sawyer; **66bl** AA/D Corrance; **66br** AA/C Sawyer; **67t** AA/C Sawyer; **68t** AA/C Sawyer; **69t** AA/C Sawyer; **70t** AA/S McBride; **71** AA/C Sawyer; **74tl** AA/P Kenward; **74/5tc** AA/S McBride; **74bl** AA/P Kenward; **74br** AA/C Sawyer; **75tr** AA/S McBride; **74/5b** AA/C Sawyer; **75br** AA/P Kenward; **76tl** AA/C Sawyer; **76tr** AA/C Sawyer; **77tl** The Frick Collection/Galen Lee; **77tr** John Bigelow Taylor/The Frick Collection; **78/9tl** AA/S McBride; **79tr** AA/C Sawyer; **79br** AA/C Sawyer; **80/1tl** AA/C Sawyer; **81tr** AA/R Elliot; **82/3** AA/P Kenward; **84t** AA/C Sawyer; **84bl** AA/C Sawyer; **84br** Harry Zernike / Museum of the City of NY; **85t** AA/C Sawyer; **86t** AA/C Sawyer; **87** AA/P Kenward; **88t** AA/C Sawyer; **89** AA/P Kenward; **92t** AA/C Sawyer; **92/3t** AA/E Rooney; **94/5t** AA/C Sawyer; **95t** AA/C Sawyer; **96t** AA/C Sawyer; **97t** AA/C Sawyer; **98** AA/P Kenward; **99t** AA/P Kenward; **100t** AA/S McBride; **101** AA/C Sawyer; **104t** AA/Nicky Lancaster; **104/5t** AA/C Sawyer; **106/7t** AA/C Sawyer; **106bl** AA/C Sawyer; **106br** AA/P Kenward; **107bl** AA/R Elliot; **107br** AA/C Sawyer; **108t** AA/S McBride; **109** AA/C Sawyer; **110/11t** AA/C Sawyer; **110tr** AA/C Sawyer; **110ctr** AA/C Sawyer; **110cbr** AA/C Sawyer; **110br** AA/S McBride; **112/3** AA/C Sawyer; **114t** AA/C Sawyer; **115** AA/S McBride; **116/7t** AA/D Corrance; **118/9t** AA/D Corrance; **120/1t** AA/D Corrance; **122/3t** AA/D Corrance; **122c** MRI Bankers' Guide to Foreign Currency, Houston, USA; **122b** AA/C Sawyer; **124/5t** AA/D Corrance; **124bl** AA; **124br** AA; **125bl** AA; **125br** AA/C Sawyer.

Every effort has been made to trace the copyright holders, and we apologise in advance for any accidental errors. We would be happy to apply the corrections in the following edition of this publication.